TAKE HEART!

You're Stronger Than You Think

Misako Yoke

Published by Author Academy Elite
PO Box 43, Powell, OH 43065
www.AuthorAcademyElite.com

Library of Congress Control Number: 2020913726

ISBN: 978-1-64746-403-5 (paperback)

ISBN: 978-1-64746-404-2 (hardback)

ISBN: 978-1-64746-405-9 (ebook)

Dear friends,

This book is not for people who are casually seeking happiness. It's for you, torn between giving up and clawing your way out.

You and I both know that life can be cruel, quite cruel at times. The world sometimes pushes us around, presses us down, and just when we've gathered up the courage to get back up, delivers another blow. That's the hardest. It could make us bitter. It could harden our hearts.

I can't begin to imagine what you are going through, but I can relate to the bitterness itself. I can feel the lump in your throat, holding back your tears. I've been there many times, and honestly, I had no idea how to bounce back.

Along my journey, countless people have shared their insights and offered guidance to help me grind out my challenges. A little wisdom goes a long way — longer than most imagine. It made me realize that I was stronger than I thought. It gave me the energy to pick myself up. It made me say, "Bring it on," again.

I didn't always "get it" straight off; I took one wrong detour after another. I made one mistake after another. I don't wish for a better past, but there are things I do wish I'd known back then. The time I wasted can't be recreated.

That's why I wrote this book. This is a book that reminds you that not only will you, too, bounce back, but you'll also tell the world to bring it on. You'll smile again. Take heart! You're stronger than you think you are. Deep down, you know it.

You've got this,
Misako

Table of Contents

Foreword
By Darren LaCroix

If you looked back at your life, what would you say your number one life lesson was? That's a deep one. Did that lesson come as a result of a struggle through adversity? The best lessons usually do. When we take the wrong detours, we can turn them into the right path for our own journey.

Right after college, I went to the American dream. I invested in my own business, a popular franchise. It seemed to be the only way to acquire a loan, even with a business partner's help. Why? Because I was right out of college and had no track record of success. The bank counted on the franchise's record of success.

I dreamed of being a multi-unit franchise owner. I did everything right. The franchise was successful. I researched locations. I spoke to other owners. I hired a lawyer to review the franchise agreement. Paying someone $100 per hour when I had little money seemed like a stretch, but I knew it was the smart thing to do. I did more homework than I ever did in school.

Fast forward a year and a half later: the franchise opened another location four miles down the road from me. On the same road with easier-parking! Yikes! My small profits faded to nil.

I ended up working 90-100 hours per week at the store and five days a week at my day job, just to stay afloat. I was mad. It just wasn't fair. The franchise should not have allowed it. Why would they do that to me? I'm a nice guy! "It's just not right," I said over and over again.

What would you do? How would you feel? I'll bet you can relate to the feeling.

I was mad at everyone else, but I realized that I was the one who had created all of my circumstances. The lawyer whom I stretched myself to pay had told me that the franchise could do that. I paid him $100 an hour and chose not to listen! Though I had no business experience, I thought I knew better. Ego. Yikes. I chose the franchise. I chose the location. I made all the decisions. I created my circumstances. I am responsible. I decided to sell my franchise at a loss and was delighted to do so.

You may wonder what happened next. This is how people introduce me now :

> *After a failed business in 1992, Darren LaCroix took the stage in a Boston comedy club and bombed miserably. It was horrible. The headliner that night told him to "keep his day job." Friends told him that his dream of making people laugh for a living was crazy and stupid. He didn't listen.*
>
> *He may have been born without a funny bone in his body, but Darren possessed the desire to learn and the willingness to fail. These were the essentials for achieving his dream. This self-proclaimed student of comedy is living proof that anything can be learned.*
>
> *Less than nine years later, in 2001, Darren LaCroix outspoke 25,000 contestants from 14 countries to become the World Champion of Public Speaking. He did it with a very funny speech. Some said it was one of the best speeches in the history of the contest.*
>
> *Since that victory, Darren travels the world, demystifying the process of creating a powerful presentation. His story*

*has inspired audiences in 45 International cities, includ-
ing faraway places like Australia, Singapore, Saudi Arabia,
China, Oman, Malaysia, and Taiwan, with his inspiration-
al journey from Chump to Champ. He is passionate about
showing people that if you are a sponge and have the right
mentors, anything is possible.*

Now, it's what I get to do for a living and teach others to
do the same.

That costly lesson and experience would be exactly what
I needed to prepare me for a bigger and better dream. Over-
coming that adversity and taking 100% responsibility was
exactly what this quiet, shy kid needed to pursue his ridicu-
lous dream of making people laugh.

If I had not been at the lowest point of my life, I would
never have tried standup, which then led me to the life I
love. If my dream had worked out, I might be owning more
retail franchises and maybe doing well by now, but would
never have found my passion. Thank God for unanswered
prayers!

So you see, failures can be our biggest assets. Can you
imagine what if I kept blaming others, though? No one really wants to hear about your problems, unless they are waiting their turn to tell you how they have it worse. They'll say,
"That's nothing . . . , etc. "

Blaming others is an easy way out. Sometimes circumstances are out of our control, but other times we put ourselves in those circumstances.

Are you confident enough to look for the role you played
in creating your circumstance? You can be blaming or fill-
ing in the hole you dug. It's like texting and driving: you are
doing one or the other or going back and forth between the

two. If we waste time blaming others, we are robbing ourselves of the very energy we need to get ourselves out of a challenge. Put all that energy on the solution.

I met Misako Yoke in 2016 when she joined my online Stage Time University. We help good presenters tell their stories and be unforgettable. Her courage, energy, and enthusiasm are infectious. I encourage many people, not all of them follow through. Misako did over and over again. When a student inspires a teacher, that gets your attention!

Misako lives a life worth watching. That's what inspires me. It's not the buff guy at the gym who motivates me to work harder; it's the person who is there for their second week still working those five-pound weights. As my mentor, Mark Brown, says, "Your life tells a story, and someone needs to hear it." You've got to live it first. The best stories come from the harshest adversity.

Let this book and the lessons from Misako's journey inspire you to keep clawing, clawing, and finding your own unique path. She'll help you turn your wrong detours into the exact path you needed to take on your journey.

Darren LaCroix
World Champion of Public Speaking
stagetimeuniversity.com

Prologue

I am a piece of bad luck.

From grade schoolteachers to corporate bosses, my ex-husband to television producers, that's what they told me back in Japan. As a woman, I was born as the worst Zodiac combination: a Fire-Horse, which only occurs once every sixty years.[1] A Fire-Horse woman can deplete her family's finances, drive her parents to an early grave, and ruin her marriage. There are some other varieties to this superstition, but the "bad luck" part is the same. You'd think this myth was put to rest in the 18th century, but it still holds its power. The birthrate in the last Fire-Horse year plummeted almost twenty-five percent from the previous year, and it jumped right back up the year after that.[2] I can think of two reasons. One, when I came into the world in the 20th century, the modern age hadn't yet arrived in Japan. Two, people were worried their Fire-Horse daughter would be treated differently — even be discriminated against. I came to realize the latter was the real reason. The society holds the Fire-Horse curse seriously.

"Oh, you, bad-luck Fire-Horse girls!" I can still hear the screaming. My seventh-grade teacher was often upset about something and blamed it on our cursed zodiac sign.

"You are such a typical Fire-Horse. You and your family will suffer!" She screamed at me when I failed to behave the way I was supposed to. She may have been a fortune-teller. Shortly after, my father's business went bust, and we fell into poverty when I was in eighth grade. My mother passed away the same year. My father broke my nose. The president of the company at my first job was murdered in front of TV cameras. It was a week after I started, and I learned it from the TV news — the company was a scam. A hoodlum almost strangled me to death on the street and stole my purse. I took a waitress job to survive, gobbled down customers' leftovers in front of the garbage bins, pretending I was tossing the food. Sometimes it was the only meal of the day. I got married, but the man left me for another woman. The first hotel I stayed overseas caught on fire. I was in American Samoa when the 2009 Tsunami hit. All my family left the earth earlier than their time. The list goes on.

"Oh, the Fire-Horse curse," some said. Some still would.

The truth is, although each unwelcome event was gut-wrenching, none of them were exclusive to me as a Fire-Horse woman. Chances are, your own experience is worse than any of mine — or all of them combined. So, why does Japan still cling to such superstitions?

You and I both know that life is full of ups and downs. Things go wrong, life gets tough, and traumatic experiences hit us without any warnings. When these things happen to us, we want to get out as soon as possible. When it happens to people we know, we don't want to see them suffer. We search for a reason — a sense of closure. For Japanese, a rare zodiac sign can serve as a seemingly harmless reason. "Oh, the Fire-Horse curse." It provides a cue to end the conversation, so we can move on. Sometimes, it did, even for me.

As you see, although it's hard to swallow, we're the ones who give meaning to the events of our lives. While we can't control everything that happens to us, we can make sense of our struggles — or try. Be it a silly superstition or a meaningful revelation, the choice is ours. It took me too long to understand that this is our one true power.

I am a Genki person.

That's who I am, and people who know me instantly understand the meaning of the word *genki* (pronounced as gain-key): lively, enthusiastic, full of energy. Sometimes my excess energy causes problems, and I have to admit that I have a little spark of insanity in me. I like the way I am. My enthusiasm is contagious, and the madness keeps me going. When life kicks my face into the mud, I make every effort to remember my strength, get back to who I am, and focus on who I'm becoming. I wasn't always this way.

I hated myself. I hated my excess energy that caused conflicts. Fitting in was one of the most critical skills to survive in Japanese society, but neither my liveliness nor enthusiasm helped. I was told, recommended, suggested to be "normal," and I tried. I knew enough about what society expected of me as a Japanese woman, so I worked hard to fit in. I sucked at everything. I ended up being victim-minded, good at wallowing, and excellent at complaining. Frustrated, I bottled up my anger and let it out on those I loved. I acted like a wimp, and I hated the way I lead my life.

It took me decades and a world trip to realize it — countless people shared their hard-earned wisdom — we are the strongest when we honor who we are. It's my turn to share those stories and insights with you.

As you read through the following chapters, I organized them using GENKI as an acronym, it's also a method I created to help you grind out adversities:

G: Get Some Breathing Room
(When Life Ambushes You)
E: Embrace Who You Are Becoming
(When You Wonder, "Now What?")
N: Navigate through Changes
(When You Start Something New and Confusing)
K: Be Kind to Yourself
(When Your Inner Voice Attacks You)
I: Integrate Who You Are with How You Live
(This Is Your Life)

You will discover how I was given the core idea of each step through my struggles, mistakes, and heartbreaks. The Genki method section is at the end of this book, and I also prepared a gift workbook for you.

No, this book won't make you invincible. Instead, you'll be prompted to take a break, recuperate, and defend yourself. You'll find yourself being *you* again, retaking charge of your life.

Genki also means "full of life" — a state well worth aspiring for. Let's make the journey together.

Chapter 1

G for Getting Some Breathing Room

"No one is so brave that he is not disturbed by something unexpected."

—Julius Caesar

What Did I Do?

The canola fields bloomed yellow under the milky spring sky, and the balmy breeze waved through the flowers.

I loved this part of Yokohama, where farmlands were preserved, thanks to the city's urban agricultural policy. It was a gentle Sunday morning in April; I was in my favorite white cardigan, on the way home from a nearby bakery. The bakery was famous for its special chocolate croissants: golden, flaky, and dipped in dark chocolate on both ends. I had scored the last two — they were also my husband's favorite.

I let out a little sigh at the apartment stoop and put my hand on the doorknob. As I opened the door, I saw my husband, all dressed up and getting his keys.

"Hey, where are you going?"

He didn't answer.

"I just got your favorite — chocolate croissants!"

He ignored my words and glided past me. I grabbed the bottom of his dark-green jacket — it looked brand-new.

He clucked his tongue. My throat tightened up, but I pushed out my words: "Wh — why have you been acting like this?" He'd ignored me for over a month.

He rolled his eyes, yanked my fingers off the jacket, and slammed the door in my face.

"What kind of jerk are you?" I smashed the bag of croissants to the floor.

My husband and I were a typical example of opposites attracting. He was analytical and reserved. I was intuitive and expressive. Bypassing the euphemisms, he was difficult for me, and I was too much as a Japanese woman. Our mutual friends and colleagues admired him for his bravery in marrying me. I was known as a restive Fire Horse: bad luck—an unruly woman.

In Japan, a 'good wife' is quiet, agreeable, and obedient, but I was none of those things. We enjoyed our differences for a while, but this changed over the years. He started furrowing his brow when I expressed my opinions, and if I didn't stop there, he took off and ignored me for the next few days.

Eventually, he would return to normal, as if nothing had happened, and soon it became our routine. Although I didn't have any idea what had caused him to give me the cold shoulder this time, I assumed it was one of those incidents. I must have said something insensitive, since he often accused me of being too opinionated and direct. However, his ignoring me had gone on too long. Also, he had started spending nights somewhere else.

"Where have you been staying lately?" I asked him a week ago. He didn't say anything, tossing his overnight duffle bag to the floor.

"Are you mad at me for something? What did I say or do?"

He sat down on the couch, picked up the remote.

"I really don't know. You have to tell me what I did wrong."

He turned on the TV.

"Hey, I'm talking to you. Look at me!" I took the remote and turned off the TV. There was silence for a moment, but he didn't look at me. He then made a phone call and started having a pleasant conversation with whoever it was. I felt like I was an invisible something—less than a human. It was clearly not working.

I realized I couldn't keep taking the same course of action and hoping for a different outcome; I decided to change my attitude first. That's the reason I rushed to the bakery before he woke up and got our favorite; it was my gesture to communicate in a better way. It should have put us in a good mood. We would have had a nice Sunday brunch, and we could have moved on to a better direction.

"Shoulda, woulda, coulda." I sighed, poured my coffee, and put the broken croissant on my plate. Alone.

Looking back, I never even tried to be a good wife by Japanese standards. Customarily, women were expected to leave the company when they got married. It was called kotobuki taisha, a congratulatory retreat from the workplace. Although kotobuki taisha was still prevalent in my era, I couldn't imagine quitting my job. It made little sense since I was getting a promotion, but I was naïve. I started to understand when I returned to work after the wedding.

A Good Wife

It was on a Monday morning right after my wedding that Mr. Watabe, founder and president of the company, summoned me. "Charisma" is the first word that comes to mind when I think of him, and he was a fierce entrepreneur. I entered his office with my steno pad, as I knew he would send me back if I didn't. Mr. Watabe was behind his desk, in a crisp shirt with the sleeves rolled up, a pen in his hand, a notepad before him. He first congratulated me on my marriage. Then he told me he was taking me off the leadership training program.

"WHY?" My voice came out as a scream, but he was still smiling, as if at a toddler. I was the only surprised one.

"Now that you've gotten married, you'll need more time at home. I don't want to wear you out," he said.

Already in the middle of the advanced leadership training, I didn't want to drop out because I got married. Held every Wednesday morning, beginning at 7 a.m., the training was hard, but I looked forward to attending each week. I was the only female in the advanced class, and Mr. Watabe was the one who put me in there.

He put his pen on the desk and laced his fingers, still smiling. "So! When is your husband planning to start a family?" His smile got even bigger.

I blinked back, lost for words. *Wait,* I thought, *does he assume that I'll give up my career? And what does he think I am, a birth-giving machine? What in the world's going on here?*

Mr. Watabe got his start in business by buying a failing restaurant and turning it into a phenomenal success. I took a waitressing job at his second restaurant, and he promoted me to his secretary at headquarters. Five years had passed since then, and the company had over forty restaurants and counting. It aimed to go public within a year. I held a position in HR then: the first and only female manager. This meant much to me.

"My marriage will not affect my performance in any way." I tried to assure him I was still the same person he'd hired, trained, and promoted.

"But think about your husband," he said. "I mean, I can't work like this without my wife's support. I don't know what she's doing at home," he chuckled, "but she takes care of things for me. She's there when I need her. Is your husband okay without the full support of his wife?"

"Absolutely. My husband is understanding," I said and meant it.

"All right then." With one elbow put on his desk, he raised his eyebrows, and I knew it was his cue; I was dismissed.

I had to admit: other married men were much more spoiled than my husband ever was. People could tell if a man was married or not by looking at him those days. He'd wear a crisp dress shirt, a clean suit with a well-chosen tie, and polished shoes. He'd have a healthy packed lunch in his briefcase. Everything was carefully prepared by his wife, who would manage all the miscellaneous tasks for him and the family. That was the norm back then, and that way, men could concentrate on work-life exclusively. My husband and I worked at the same company. I saw him being teased by colleagues and bosses about his wife stubbornly working full time. I was glad he didn't seem to take it seriously.

I shouldn't have been surprised when my husband began to point out my sloppy housework. I couldn't ask him to share house chores without getting into a huge fight. He demanded that I shift my focus to supporting him. I hated it, but it made sense: even though we were at the same level as managers, his salary was way more than mine. That indicated a glass ceiling for further promotion for me, as a woman. That's the way it was. Maybe I should have been the one to step down, but I didn't want to. Soon, I started feeling that I had two bosses — one at work and one at home. If I wasn't performing well at the office, Mr. Watabe would demote me at once. If I didn't do the housework properly, my husband would push me to quit my job. I was frustrated doing dishes while my husband got ready for training. I feared that when I attended the seminar, I'd be ill-prepared for the topic.

On top of everything, I had two inner voices fighting. One encouraged me to grind through until my husband understood how important it was for me. The other kept screaming, "Look around you. The whole society is designed for men to work. Don't you get it? That's the way it is. Grow up!" The argument in my head never ended, which added additional stress. I became irritable all the time, and I often took my anger out on my subordinates. As the IPO process progressed, the workload was getting heavier and heavier. Juggling work and household chores were getting out of control, but I still didn't want to give up. I ended up dropping the ball and cost the company a considerable amount of money. I resigned in shame.

My husband left the company soon after. I could easily imagine his boss judging him based on his mistake—he couldn't make me quit. Others must have teased him, making jokes about everything I'd done. Even so, my husband didn't blame me at all, and while I was grateful, I always felt guilty about what I'd done to his career. I also feared I may have proven a married woman should follow the social norm, stepping down to support her husband. This was truly painful, rocked my mind to the very core.

It was hard to change jobs in Japan in those days. My husband went back to school to get his CPA, and I became a temp to support both of us until he found a decent position. The temp work didn't pay much. I often had odd jobs on the side until an I.T. company gave me an offer for full-time employment.

The company had more women, including married ones. I loved achieving goals as a team, learning new skills, and applying them to improve productivity. I took business courses and language classes after work. It was working well until my husband completed his CPA and got hired by a major firm. His new job was demanding, and he started mentioning how little support he was getting from his wife. *Here we go again,* I thought. I'd stepped back into quicksand.

Tick-Tock

"I guess I never was a good wife." I finished the second croissant.

Tick tock, tick tock.

Our clock was a loud one—even louder lately since I was alone a lot. I hated it, but there were so many things to be done before replacing that stupid clock. Sunday often slipped away between catching up and preparing, sighing and grunting.

Just as the annoying clock struck 4:00 p.m., my husband came back.

"You're back." I didn't know what else to say.

"Yeah," he said, still standing at the entrance.

"Where did you go?" He didn't answer, but came into the living room and sat down. I assumed that he was searching for the words for an apology for his attitude, or to complain about whatever I'd done. I was preparing to fight back if he went that way.

"There's someone else," he said.

I stood up.

"Wha—Who is—How—When did—" The words all stuck in my throat. He buried his face into his palms. People say, "A wife always knows," but that wasn't true in my case. I didn't think he would ever cheat. He wasn't that kind of person. *Or was he? Did I even know him?* My mind started spinning, and my knees became wobbly. I leaned against the wall.

Tick tock, tick tock.

My husband's face was still in his palms, his shoulders were shaking, and he was crying. Watching this display, I grew cold, and anger grew inside me.

"What exactly is going on here?" I spat the words. From our past, I knew I should wait until he was ready to talk, but knowing and doing were two different matters.

Tick tock, tick tock—the clock sounded like a time bomb. My stomach clenched. I needed to end this, so I went for the deepest question.

"Do you want to save this marriage?"

He pulled his head up and wiped his eyes. Then, he looked at me, forlornly. He parted his lips as if to speak, but then he closed his mouth again. He straightened his chin, he took a deep breath, and he shook his head. "No, I don't."

***

When I came home from work on Monday, he had already moved out. His side of the closet was empty, his books were gone, and so were his knickknacks. He didn't take the annoying tick-tocking clock that had been there for the past six years. I ripped it off the wall and hurled it to the floor. A battery popped out from the plastic compartment, rolled to the corner of the room, and stopped. So did the clock.

It was a wedding gift from a boss. At our wedding, he'd said, "You will never guess how marriage is like a canoe trip." He was partially right. My husband had jumped off abruptly, so the vessel capsized. My pride was swept away, while regrets, doubts, disappointments, shame, and anger bobbed around me. Some clung to my body, as festering seaweed.

"You cheated AND ignored me for a month!" I grabbed a cushion and swung at the couch. "What kind of coward are you?" I ripped off the window treatment. I stalked around the room and grabbed the vase, the tea set, the framed pictures, the candy bowl—and smashed them into smithereens. Anger fuels itself. I kicked the *fusuma* sliding door, full force. Composed of a light wooden frame covered with thick papers, *fusuma* are a common room divider in Japanese houses. The frame broke, and I fell into it. As my fingers touched the long strands of fiber, eerily familiar senses crept over my skin. The memory had been buried for a long time, but I began to picture myself on the broken *fusuma* before. *Did I fall into it?* No, I was kicked. *Who kicked me so hard?*

Now the back of my hand felt sticky with blood. I was sixteen years old, and it was my blood.

The Winter

I remembered that it had been a cold February night. Dad and I were sitting at our chabudai, a short-legged round table for dinner in the corner of a shabby house. Each of us had a bowl of rice, pickled daikon radish, grilled mackerel, and miso soup in a small wooden bowl. A simple supper was all I'd prepared. There was also a half-gallon bottle of *sake* liquor and a smudged glass at Dad's side. Dad sipped his soup and sighed.

"I miss your mom's cooking. Oh, I miss her so much." He poured *sake* into his glass and chugged it. He'd been drinking too much—as if he was trying to drown himself. Mom had been gone for two years at the time.

On an early February afternoon, Mom said she had a little headache. By midnight, it had gotten worse, so Dad brought her to the emergency room. The doctor told us that he needed to run some tests. Mom came back on the following Sunday in a plain urn with the scent of snow.

Dad used to be a funny, witty, and a never-give-up type of business owner. He spoiled his family: we had a personal driver, housekeepers, and often professional landscapers worked on the gardens. Our house sat on the hill, adjacent to a wildlife protection area with views of the Tanzawa mountain range in the distance. I still remember the early summer afternoon. The breeze swayed lilac trees in full bloom, carried the fragrant air through the living room where Mom was playing her polished ebony grand piano. Her delicate fingers danced over the keys; the piano notes faded into a mulberry field in the back of the house.

When I turned fourteen, his company made a downturn, but we weren't worried. In the past, Dad bounced back quickly, and we believed it was another one of his "hiccups." Everything changed when Dad's business partner, also a good friend, committed suicide. In the chaos of the tragedy, something snapped in Dad. He lost his endless energy and with it his business. We lost our home as well, and it was Mom's dream house.

We also had to sell as much as possible, and Mom's piano was the first one to go. On the day a delivery company would take it away, she played Schubert's "Impromptu No.3" early in the morning. When I heard the piano, I ran downstairs to jump on the stool with her, as I always did, but I stopped in the hallway. Mom always had a calm smile on her face, no matter what came her way. She was like a mountain lily, graceful, even in the rain, but the Mom I knew wasn't there. There was a pale, sunken-cheeked woman reflected on the well-polished piano lid, and I couldn't believe she was my mother. Schubert's "Impromptu No.3" is a calm piece, and she always played tenderly, but I never imagined the piece could express such sorrow. I wondered if Mom was crying through the piano, or her piano was crying for her — I went back to my room. All the autumn colors were gone, and the views from my window seemed bleak.

We then sold my cherry blossom kimono, which Mom purchased for my *Shichi-Go-San*, a traditional rite of passage. Dad's Japanese sword, walnut bookshelves, and his desk were the next. Many books, my brother's vintage ship models, almost everything we adored was taken away. Our dog ate something poisonous and died while we were in the chaos of moving out. The boxes full of our family pictures went missing during the move. We roamed around, often stayed in the car, and, in December, finally settled into a low-income house next to a town cemetery. The house was old, didn't have a fridge, the doors hung crooked, and drafts blew through everywhere. Mom didn't let us give up, and she always managed to make us cling to a sliver of hope. "We'll grind it through. That's what we do the best," we believed every time she said. "If Winter comes, can Spring be far behind?" It was one of Mom's favorite poems[3].

Then, she passed away abruptly — that was the biggest hit, and we didn't take it well. My brother Takuya and Dad got into a fistfight at Mom's funeral, and Takuya fled. Dad took the steepest downhill turn from there. That energetic, ambitious, and relentlessly enthusiastic Dad couldn't be found anywhere in him.

Dad eventually took a long-distance driver's job, and we moved into a small house near the truck rental, far away from my high school. He took long-distance routes quite often, came home exhausted. Desperately lonely, I wished that Dad would stay with me more, but my mouth almost always spewed rude words at him as an angry teenager. The funny thing about my anger: it did prevent me from crumbling down like Dad. It gave me feelings of strength, however false, that pushed me through the pain. Anger also blocked me from imagining the excruciating torment Dad had been enduring after the series of events stripped him of everything that he was.

Here we were, in a small old shack: everything was tainted with poverty — it was hard to accept how much had been taken away from us. When Dad said he missed her, my intention was to share our feelings. "Me too, Dad. I miss Mom, too." That was what I was going to say. My teenage mind, however, was stubborn. Dad missing Mom's miso soup hurt me. Mom was a fantastic cook, and I always thought I'd learn her skills in the future. I was trying to recreate her taste, but it was a great struggle for a teenager who'd grown up spoiled. It was a painful reminder that time hadn't healed our wounds like it was supposed to. So I scoffed at Dad and turned my head.

"THAT'S IT." Dad trashed the table. He then grabbed me by the collar and shoved me away. While I was trying to regain my balance, he kicked my back, and I smashed into the *fusuma* sliding door, breaking its fragile frame.

"YOU STUPID, SPOILED BRAT." He kicked my stomach. I coughed and curled up.

"YOU HAVE NO IDEA! NO IDEA AT ALL!" Another kick struck my shins.

"NO SNAPPY COMEBACK, HUH? COME ON, STAND UP. GIVE IT A SHOT! HUH?" He was hammered, and I was provoked. I got up on my hands.

"YOU SHOULDN'T HAVE BEEN BORN!" His foot met my nose and lips, and I saw stars. I tasted iron. Blood flowed down my chin and dropped onto the *fusuma*. I looked up at Dad, who'd frozen at the sight of his daughter covered in blood. Tearing outside, I ran and ran, until I realized that I wasn't wearing shoes in the winter street. I was telling myself, "Don't cry now. Don't let yourself grow weak. Don't cry now, don't cry. You are the one to be strong!" Someone once told me this, and I often repeated it whenever I wanted to cry. I couldn't remember who said it, but I feared that if I started to cry, I'd collapse in the night in the middle of winter. I couldn't afford to let that happen. "Don't let yourself grow weak, don't, don't, don't..." I repeated.

Mr. Riptides

I surprised a friend, Nanami, by showing up with a bloody face and bare feet. She gasped and pulled me into her apartment, screaming, "My God, that skinny bastard did this to you again!" She didn't mean my dad. I was dating an explosive boy, and he once punched me in front of her. She assumed that it had been him. We'd broken up long ago, but I couldn't tell her it was my dad who'd done it to me.

Nanami's little studio apartment was warm, and a few empty plates and a teacup were still on the table by her bed. She sat me down on her couch and brought over a bottle of rubbing alcohol and a few cotton balls.

"It's going to sting a bit . . ." She applied rubbing alcohol, wiped around my lips, and on the side of my right eye.

"Looks like it's going to bruise." She pointed at my nose. I felt a throbbing pain in my nose each time my heart pumped.

"Are you hurt anywhere else? Cold? Hungry? Thirsty?" She looked at me and said, "You must still be in shock. Oh, it's high time you dumped that stupid guy! You deserve more than him, you know?" She brought over a blanket and wrapped it around me. "Oh," she said, went back to the bathroom and brought a wet towel, wiped my feet. "There. Much better. Now, put your feet into the blanket, keep them cozy." She patted my feet.

Nanami was in her early thirties and a pâtisserie at a local bakery where I was working after school. She taught me how to fry donuts to a golden brown, fill pastries with cream, and drizzle chocolate over crispy croissants. She was sweet as a pastry herself—warm like a fresh-baked croissant—and her hair and eyes were chestnut-colored, lighter brown than mine. We quickly became close. She lived by herself near my house, and would often invite me over for supper, knowing that I was alone a lot. We learned that both of our names were ocean-related. A Japanese name can be written with a variety of characters with different meanings. Her parents had chosen "a child of the seven seas" for her name. For mine, Misako, my parents chose "water and sand; a child of the shore." Many parents name their children in hopes that their kids will grow accordingly. Both of our parents seemed to wish for us to receive bountiful blessings from the ocean, sail beyond the horizon, and embrace life's challenges. I'm not sure if our names somehow affected our personalities, but we both had dreams of exploring overseas. She told me that she was planning to attend a culinary school in France when she'd saved enough money. It looked like she was making progress—on her table were school brochures and paperwork written in French.

"I'm so sorry I dropped in like this." My lips hurt when I spoke.

"Oh, don't be silly! I'm glad you came. You stay here tonight, okay?" I nodded. She assumed that my dad was away again, and that's the reason I'd come to her. I still couldn't find the words to explain, as the whole thing felt surreal. Dad never even raised his voice at me before.

"So, do you wanna talk about what happened?" Nanami asked, but I shook my head.

"Do you want me to give him a lesson? I can throw that skinny guy into the dough mixer, easy. Look!" She showed me her biceps, and I put my forehead against her arm. It felt nice to have someone to lean on.

"All right then." She patted my head and turned on the TV. There was a comedy show that featured a laugh track every few seconds. The characters were on a fake beach, surrounded by the sound of seagulls and mighty waves in the distance.

"Do you still remember how funny Mr. Riptide was on the beach?" she asked.

Mr. Riptide was the owner of the bakery we both worked for. He was also the chief baker, probably around fifty, wiry, with tan-colored skin and a bright smile under the baker's hat. The toque was often crooked, as its owner would often fail to duck through the kitchen door. I remembered when he arranged a group trip to Isshiki beach, a forty-minute drive from the bakery. It had been midsummer, the sun blasting the sand and setting the ocean aglitter. The soft breeze passing through the pine trees . . . everything came rushing back. The baker grew up near the beach, and he knew everything about it. The beautiful lawn area on the little hill, the tidepools, and the best *umi-no-ie*, seasonal restaurants on the beach. He shared everything that only the locals would know. He warned us about the riptides and where to avoid them.

"If you're caught," he said, "don't try to swim straight back to shore. You'll only exhaust yourself. You need to escape from it by swimming horizontally to the beach."

He moved his arms as if he were swimming. "It's not easy, so the best thing to do is shout and get the attention of the lifeguards," he said. "To do so, you've got to focus on three things. Stop. Breathe. Channel your inner Samurai."

"Your inner Samurai?" Nanami chuckled.

"Asking for help doesn't require a Samurai-mind, does it?"

"Oh, you don't know a thing!" He responded with confidence. "Asking for help requires guts. Watch now. Stop. Breathe. Channel your inner Samurai and scream." He inhaled and let out a big roar, "HELP!"

"That doesn't sound like a Samurai warrior at all!" someone said in a teasing voice.

"Oh, don't underestimate the power of riptides!" He raised his arms and started chasing us. Everyone laughed and scattered as he shouted, "Run! Run for your life! Mr. Riptide's gonna get you! Mr. Riptide's gonna get you!" He kept chasing us until we were all rolled onto the warm and soft sand, gasping for air from the laughter. After that, we started calling him "Mr. Riptide," and he seemed to like it.

Nanami mimicked him chasing us, and a laugh track played with perfect timing. I wanted to laugh but winced from the pain instead. She looked at me with her warm smile.

"Ah, Mr. Riptide. A funny, funny guy." She chuckled, fixed my blanket, then brought pajamas and a pillow for me. "I need to be at the bakery by 5:00 a.m. for my dough, but you should stay and sleep in, Misako. All right?"

I nodded.

As she turned off the lights, I was thinking about the day on the beach—the sounds of the waves, the warmth of the sand underfoot, and the scent of sunscreen. I was rolling and laughing with others. It seemed so very far away from where I was—in all senses.

Nanami's alarm went off at four, and she quickly got ready for work.

"Sorry I woke you up so early. Go back to sleep, but, oh . . ." She came close to the couch and hunched down.

"Promise me you'll stay here until your dad comes home,

okay? He's coming home today, right?" I said yes, but it was a lie. Dad was about to leave for another long-distance delivery trip this morning. I was still too confused. If my nose hadn't been pulsing from the pain, I would have thought it was a bad dream.

"You should lie low today. Sometimes the best thing to do is rest. Give it time to heal. Okay?" She waved and turned the lights off, closing her apartment door. I heard her rhythmic footsteps fading away. I got up and peeked outside through her aluminum blinds. She walked out onto the street, and the street lights cast an orange glow on her black coat. She turned toward the station and disappeared. I decided to go home, putting on clothes, along with Nanami's jacket and shoes. The jacket was too long for me, but it was the warmest garment I'd ever worn.

***

I lived in a sleepy town that was even quieter at five o'clock in the dark winter morning. Dad usually left around 4:30 for a long-distance delivery, no matter how drunk he'd gotten the night before. Then, he wouldn't come home for at least a week, sometimes a couple of weeks. *It should give us time to cool down,* I thought.

"Oh, no." I stopped. Dad's beaten up truck was still there, under a flickering street light. I hid in the overgrown bushes between the truck and the house without thinking. From the frozen bush, I gazed at the sky and found Venus, the Morning-star. A meteor shot across the sky and disappeared. My fingers and toes had grown numb, and I was shivering. I started to think about going back to Nanami's but noticed that the kitchen light was on. A silhouette appeared behind the frosted kitchen window, moved around, and then, everything blended into the dark again. Dad was leaving. The squeaky door opened and closed. His key chain jingled. He had a habit of dragging his heels, and the sound had never seemed louder. I put my elbow to my mouth and tried to stop shivering. *Shhh-clop, shhh-clop.* The sound kept coming closer. *I couldn't be found — not like this,* I thought, but I couldn't think of anything else but closing my eyes. The sound moved past me and faded. Dad's truck started after a couple of coughing sounds, and then silence returned.

I let out a big sigh, got out from the bushes, and reached for the doorknob. Dad hadn't locked the door. Inside, all the dishes were on the dish rack, and the floor and table were wiped clean. There was the broken *fusuma* door, propped in the dingy room's far corner. I approached it and traced my bloodstains on the *fusuma* paper.

Many years had passed, but my fingertips remembered the feel of the sullied strands of fiber.

Cape Inubo

I looked around the living room that I'd trashed. I closed my eyes, and I felt a big lump forming in my throat — one that threatened to choke me. And then, I couldn't hold the word any longer. "Mom . . ." Tears trickled down my cheeks, carrying away my energy. "What should I do now? I miss you, Mom.

Why did you have to leave us so soon?" I hugged my knees and cried until a headache's vice grip subdued me.

I was in the car, headed to the lighthouse on Cape Inubo, where I was born in a nearby hotel room during my parents' summer vacation. It was my parents' favorite story that I'd come into the world on the first day of their vacation, four weeks before the due date. A midwife had been staying at the hotel and helped them.

The lighthouse is perched on the easternmost tip of Japan's main island, and the cape sticks out into the Pacific. Below the lighthouse, hostile crags jut out over the vast sea. The wind howls and waves echo, crashing into the cliffside — clearly audible from a distance.

I drove through the town and entered the parking lot under heavy fog near the lighthouse. I kept driving. There were warning signs everywhere.

DO NOT ENTER.
STOP.
NO U-TURN BEYOND THIS POINT.

I ignored all of them.

"No, I don't." My husband had made it clear that he didn't want me to be in his life.

"YOU SHOULDN'T HAVE BEEN BORN!" *Maybe Dad had been right*, I thought. I chuckled as the car was approaching the last fence. I gripped the steering wheel and gathered up all my strength to slam down the accelerator.

The car broke through the fence and arched into gray space above the whitecaps. I don't remember the impact when the car hit the water's surface, but I remember the feeling of overwhelming calmness under the stormy ocean. The car was sinking vertically, and it was complete darkness in front of me. I pulled myself through the window and looked up. The surface was already high above me. Air bubbles from my clothes made spheres and rushed toward the surface.

"Come with us, come with us," the bubbles whispered, leaving me.

I raised my left arm and felt the air pockets climbing over my skin. I opened my fingers and felt the last remnant of hope pull away. The water above me became perfect blue. Below me was an abyss.

What is this? Something was swimming toward me, getting closer. It was a tall, wiry man, somewhat familiar-looking, but I couldn't remember who he was. I tried to swim away. The surrounding water was heavy, and my arms were even heavier. Hair plastered my face. I started to panic, and the man grabbed my left arm and shouted, "Misako!"

***

I woke up on the broken *fusuma*, panting, and soaked in sweat. A gleam of light came from the window as a car passed by.

It was one of my recurring dreams of falling, but in the past, I'd always woken up before the car hit the water. I noticed that my left arm still felt as if someone had given it a hard pull. Not only that, but I could also hear a sharp voice. I knew who he was.

After the incident, Dad started taking the longest delivery routes. *What if Dad decided to abandon me?* Although I was scared, I couldn't tell anyone about the situation. Pretending things were okay was the only armor I had to protect my open wounds. I feared that if I took off the armor, I'd bleed out and never get up. As a typical teenager, I hated the idea of getting sympathy or, worse, pity. I needed to believe I could survive by myself. At least I had a house to come home to, and the bakery's leftovers fed me well enough. I thought I could make it to high school graduation, but the bakery started donating the leftovers to charity. I needed to come up with something to preserve the illusion of wellness.

I was working the bakery's latest shift, and almost everything had sold out that day. Mr. Riptide came to the store and looked around at the empty shelves.

"Looks like we don't have anything for the charity today, do we?" He smiled. I smiled back and asked him if I could take extra shifts. In my calculation, it was doable and could reduce my fear of going to sleep on an empty stomach.

"Oh?" he said and looked me in the eye. He tilted his head, saying, "Okay, come with me."

We went to the kitchen. He sat in front of the stainless baking counter and gestured for me to sit on a stool next to him. The kitchen was clean and empty, filled with a lovely, buttery scent.

"All right. What's really going on here? You still need time for your homework, don't you?" I didn't know how to explain it. He kept looking into my eyes, but eventually, his eyebrows flattened, and he let out a sigh.

"Uh-oh. I know that look. You can't tell me, huh?" He nodded. "You're not the first one, you know? Why do bad things happen to good people? That's the question." He tapped his chin with his index finger, and then kneaded between his eyebrows.

"Okay. I'll tell you what," he said.

"Kitchen work is a bit harder, but I think you can handle it. What do you say?" He offered me a promotion to become an assistant baker. I would get better wages than being a cashier.

I nodded.

"Okay, then. You can still have time for your homework," he said with a wink. I wrinkled my nose, and he patted my shoulder.

On my first day as part of the kitchen staff, Mr. Riptide showed me how to operate the mixing machine. It roared and rumbled and scared me to death. As I took a few steps back, he grabbed my left arm and pulled me in front of him. Then he said, "Do you remember what I said about the riptide?" I nodded and said, "Stop. Breathe. Channel your inner Samurai."

He smiled and said, "Yup. You've got this, Misako. You are not the dough being beaten up. You are in charge here; the machine works for you. Separate yourself from the noise. All right? Be a samurai," he said.

I completed the task and brought the dough to the proofer cabinet. I went back to the machine for the next batch, and I heard "Misako!" It was the chief baker working at the kneading table. He gave me a flour-dusted thumbs up and smiled. I smiled back, and I was proud. It was probably the first time I got the sense of my own accomplishment.

Dad never gave up on me, and we came to terms. He gave me plenty of chances to recognize that I loved him more than I hated what he'd done to me. Our wounds never disappeared, but time did lessen our pains.

Mr. Riptide came to my rescue, I thought, taking a deep breath. I sat up, tucked my chin, and rolled my shoulders back as if the roaring machine was in front of me.

If the sixteen-year-old Misako survived that situation, this should be nothing. That was clear. I peeled myself up, went to bed, and wrapped myself in a blanket, just as Nanami had done for me.

Then I thought she said, "Sometimes, the best thing to do is rest. Give it time to heal. Okay?"

Chapter 2

E for Embracing Who You Are Becoming

"Above all, be true to yourself, and if you cannot put your heart in it, take yourself out of it."

— Anonymous

Tuesday in Yokohama

Smacking the alarm clock, jumping right out of bed, running into the shower. Everything was automatic until I stepped out and wiped off the foggy mirror. I didn't like what I saw: dark circles under my eyes, puffed-up eyelids, and a drooping mouth. I rolled my eyes, wrapped myself in a towel, and went to the kitchen, only to realize the coffeemaker was missing. I thought my ex-husband would have left it, but apparently, he liked the morning coffee as much as I did. I shook my head, gulped a big glass of water, and started getting ready for work. The living room was still a mess, so I tiptoed through broken bits of my past-life on the way to the door.

The city's business district was bustling as usual. Many were picking up coffee from shops; some were sitting at the counter seats; some were eating breakfast. Roll doors were clanking open—a dry cleaning business, a pharmacy, a small general store—the typical routine.

It was just another morning in Yokohama, where I'd been commuting for years. I trotted down the streets among other commuters as if we all were on a conveyor belt.

The elevator doors opened to a world of gray: rows of desks, fluorescent lamps, bleak and familiar—my floor.

I pushed the heavy gray door that led to the women's locker room.

"Oh no, you came to work?" Akiko widened her dark, warm brown eyes. My best friend knew everything.

"I didn't want to be at home today." I tossed my bag into my locker and headed to the office. I sat down in my chair, turned on the PC, and stared at the login page. The reflection of my face on the screen was telling me one word: pathetic.

Akiko came to my desk, holding two cups of coffee.

"I thought you could use this." She handed me one.

"Thanks," I mumbled and kept staring at the screen. Akiko had the energy of a hummingbird. She was either running with her natural bouncy hair in sync, or furiously typing at her keyboard, or escorting a client to the conference room. We had always shared enthusiasm for life, fueling each other's hearts. Usually, I looked forward to our morning chat, but now I couldn't even look at her. She patted my shoulder and headed to her seat. I heard her rhythmic typing, and others started calling the prospects.

As I looked up, the sales team headed to the door, and many were tackling their tasks. It was comforting to hear and see their routine. It was like a reminder that even though my world had crumbled around me, I was a part of a bigger world that was still functioning. I typed my password into the system and checked my to-do list. It was long. Now that no one was going to give me the cold shoulder if I stayed late at the office, I could devote all my energy to work, I realized — one less thing to be worried about. I'd use the work as my cane to move forward.

Opting for the fastest way to settle the divorce, I was officially single two weeks later. Everything was back to normal. At least that's what I thought.

Chizuko was making a fresh pot of coffee when I walked into the office's kitchenette. Her cat-eyes contained a smile as she turned.

"Almost ready," she said, and then lowered her voice. "You're not going to the party, are you?"

"What party?" I frowned.

"That stupid party being thrown by those HR girls. It says *Cheer-Up Party for Misako*. What are they thinking?" She shook her head and rolled her eyes.

I knew nothing about it until Chizuko told me.

"Cheer-up party, huh? Are they going to bring me a new husband?" I lifted my eyebrow and chuckled, but Chizuko wasn't amused.

"Don't be silly. You don't want a rebound guy. Besides, you can't remarry for six months anyway, remember?"

Japanese law allowed men to remarry the day after a divorce, but women had to remain single for half a year in my era.

"Isn't that one of the stupidest laws?" I said. I wasn't sure if I should tell her I wasn't even invited. At any rate, I had noticed the HR staff acting differently after I sent in my marital paperwork. They abruptly ended conversations when I walked through their section. I caught someone shushing once. "Shh, shh, look who's coming." It was apparent that they were chit-chatting about my "misfortune." I realized that I'd become a *batsu-ichi*, roughly translated as a "strike one," commonly used in reference to divorcées. As everyone knows, gossip has a short life span, so I figured that someone else would do something gossip-worthy, soon enough. *Not a big deal,* I thought. I was wrong.

"Do you have an hour after work today?" The head of HR, Mr. Hayada, called on my extension. He was tall, gaunt, saturnine, and known for his cutting sarcasm. Imagining him tapping his long, bony fingers on a table frightened many. I'd given him a nickname: Mr. Bony-fingers. I barely managed a simple "yes."

"Splendid," he said. "Could you meet me at the lounge in Isezaki Washington Hotel at six, please?" He hung up without waiting for my answer. I must have done something wrong, so the head of H.R. needed to talk in person outside the office building. I knew I was sloppy at paperwork since I despised those meaningless, outdated, privacy-invasive questionnaires. Was my paperwork *that* bad, though? I let out a big sigh.

The Question

Isezaki Washington Hotel was located next to Isezaki Park. Magnolia trees lined both sides of the park, shooting up new leaves into June's evening sky. The hotel's big windows were filled with the tender green. Mr. Hayada was already at a table, looking out. He noticed me and notified the waiter with a nod.

"Thank you for joining me. Let's have some beer." He ordered two tall glasses of beer. I didn't want to have a beer, but I said, "Thank you," to be polite.

"You know, your misfortune. I'm so sorry to hear that, first of all." He pushed his glasses back up his nose.

"I appreciate it, but it was my decision as well. I'm fine with it."

"So—" He stopped as the beer arrived. The waiter left, but he didn't restart right away. He had a way of making everyone uncomfortable with prolonged silences.

"Well." He raised his drink, and I did, too. I watched the bubbles forming at the bottom of our glasses. The bubbles rushed to the top, only to get stuck in the foamy head. The froth collapsed as Mr. Hayada's nose touched it.

"As you know, we've been open to hiring married women and very happy with their performances." I nodded. He took another sip.

"To the best of my knowledge, we don't have any experience working with a divorced woman. You may be the very first." He twisted the right corner of his thin lips.

"I 'may be' the very first" part bothered me. He might be implying something I was afraid of. Japanese companies, especially large ones, rarely fired their employees in those days. It was almost a social taboo. Instead, they made it hard for the undesirable employee to remain motivated, subtly suggesting a better way—voluntary resignation. I've seen those cases where workers were left with little to do besides staring out the windows, often in a warehouse corner or small dark office space. It was called *madogiwa zoku*, or window seat tribe—kept on the payroll without a second chance. With the bubble economy long gone, some would settle for the honorless position, enduring it until the mandatory retirement age, which was sixty. I wondered if Mr. Hayada was announcing that I'd become an undesirable employee, to see if I got the message without him needing to say anything too obvious. I felt my stomach drop.

"Your divorce shook the department of HR quite a bit, you know?" His mouth twitched again.

"If you are worried about my performance, let me assure you that my divorce will not affect my performance in any way." I felt a jolt of pain saying it. I had used the same phrase right after getting married, except for the word "divorce."

"Your boss told me you're a reliable member of the team." He took another sip of beer and continued. "That doesn't matter. As the head of HR, I'm not sure how to report your case to the headquarters," he said calmly.

I was relieved to hear my boss valued me and disappointed to hear that it didn't matter to the head of the HR department. *Then, what is it?*

"Um . . . What do you want me to do, Mr. Hayada?" I wasn't sure if I'd hidden my irritation well enough.

"Oh, no. I wouldn't say anything about what you should or shouldn't do. I'm sure you will figure it out," he said. We both took a sip in bitter silence.

"Well, I must let you be. Whatever you decide, let me know." He took the bill and stood up.

"Thank you for the beer," I said to Mr. Hayada's back.

Reading between the lines is a critical skill for Japanese, but it's never been my forte. I did sense that Mr. Hayada was telling me that my divorce was an unwelcome event in his department. *He didn't say it, but he might be uprooting me from my current department and putting me into the window seat tribe. Is it true? Or is he hoping that I quit voluntarily? How can I be sure?* My mind started spinning, and I felt dizzy.

"Stop. Breathe. Channel your inner Samurai . . ." It was my mantra these days. I said it in my mind and took a long, deep breath until every corner of my lungs was packed with fresh oxygen. Then I slowly let it go. Eventually, I realized that there was no use in continuing to think about Mr. Hayada's mind. I left the lounge and walked into the park. The evening breeze blew through the branches, tossing young leaves in the twilight.

I was lucky to build a good relationship with colleagues, and some of them became my close friends. Akiko was my partner, Satoka was a system engineer, and Chizuko was in the systems testing section—those were my closest friends at the company. We often gathered at lunchtime, and that day, we were at the corner of the conference room.

"So, how was the beer with Mr. Bony-fingers?" Akiko asked me as we finished up eating.

"No way! You had a beer with him? WHY?" Suddenly, the room was like a microwave, popcorn popping inside. Satoka was always calm, almost imperturbable, but even she widened her eyes and said, "Whoa." Chizuko asked, "Why did you torture yourself after all you've been through?"

I closed my eyes, tapping my fingers on the table, and said,

"So . . ." in a gloomy voice and kept silent. We all burst into laughter.

"What did he want, anyway?" Satoka asked.

"He didn't say what he wanted of me, although I got the message: I became an 'obstacle' to his job," I said.

"You're not leaving the company, are you?" Chizuko asked. I said no way, and then Akiko asked, "So . . . is that what you want to do?"

"What do you mean?" I asked.

"I'm just curious. Now that you're free, you can do anything you want, right?"

Akiko was known to throw out profound questions nonchalantly.

"Ouch, I don't really know," I said.

She looked into my eyes, waiting for my answer. I couldn't find any, and it surprised me. Everyone was now waiting for my answer, so I replied, "You know I love jokes. Should I crack one now?"

"Aw, no! Not now!" Someone said, everyone laughed, and lunch hour was over.

I went back to work on presentation slides for my sales team. I was a sales administrator—one of the people in the background. When clients arrived, I would escort them to a booked conference room, make some coffee, and serve all parties present. I would quickly check to see if anyone on the team wanted me to bring an extra pen or paper or whatever. After the meeting concluded, I would take care of the used cups, clean the whiteboard, and straighten the chairs for the next session.

I shared the feeling of accomplishment when the sales team achieved their goals. Most of them treated me well. I was always thinking about how to be more productive. I proposed to use a housekeeping service, instead of us women washing cups and emptying trash cans every evening. My division boss helped me to present the idea to the HR. He also gave me a promotion, but there was an obvious glass ceiling he could do nothing about. One of the sales managers spat at my face: "spare me the gender equality crap, will you?" I knew he wasn't the only one who thought of me as a restive horse.

Shortly after, the company hired a housekeeping service. It was announced as the HR's idea, which stung a bit, but I was busy looking for something new to achieve.

I needed to continue moving forward as if I were a bicycle. Keeping busy was adequate anesthesia for the pain my ex-husband had inflicted, and it also helped with the overwhelming feelings of worthlessness. However, I started noticing that tingling sensation you get when the anesthetic wears off.

Is this really what I want to do? When I thought about it, my head shook, as if my muscles knew me better than my brain. My other voice screamed at me: *That's not how I want to lead my life, now is it?* I didn't have an answer for it, and that scared me the most. I was too busy getting approval, neglecting myself, my life.

Mt. Karamatsu

The 6:35 a.m. highway bus from Tokyo drove through
low-hanging clouds. It arrived at Hakuba Valley Terminal on
time, ten minutes before noon. Hakuba is known for its world-
class ski resorts and having hosted the Nagano Winter Olym-
pics in the 90s. It's also one of Japan's most well-known trekking destinations in the summer.

I found a pack of *oyaki* dumplings, the regional cuisine, at a
local store. I remembered my big brother Takuya loved them —
I'd come here to see him. He was working on one of the trails
and helping maintain some mountain huts.

Takuya once made himself a successful accountant at a
large firm in Tokyo. Although everyone admired his success,
he grew more depressed as each year passed by. He started
drinking, and the binges became longer and longer. He ended
up hospitalized from heavy drinking twice in one month and
was unable to continue his job at the firm. He took a long back-
packing trip, then dropped everything, and left the city to join
a mountain trail maintenance team. When he came to town to
resupply, he would call me, and we'd have dinner together. He
looked happier and healthier every time we met. I wanted to
know how he'd bounced back and beyond: from the room full
of empty *sake* bottles to a sky station, working with vigor — and
smiling.

The cable car at the bottom of the mountain flew through

swirling mists. Next came a chair lift, and soon I had to squint my eyes: a panorama of snow-draped peaks contrasting with the deep-blue sky came into view. I was gliding above the verdant slopes, my shadow following ten feet beneath me. The clanking sounds got closer, and so did my shadow. I then hopped down from the lift and followed the other hikers. I took the trail to a little alpine pond that mirrored the mountains and the sky. Legend has it that a dragon lives deep in the pond; there was a small shrine to keep it calm. Most day-hikers would enjoy the area and return, but I continued up into the mountain. The trail got steeper, then followed a knife-edge along the ridge with steep drop-offs. A frozen white river ran through a narrow valley, hundreds of feet below. A wisp of clouds appeared as I gained elevation, and soon I found myself walking in dense fog.

As I carefully proceeded, traversing the rocky sections, I was thinking about Takuya. Everything seemed to be quite the opposite of what he'd had in the city: the speed, the convenience, the noises. I also remembered how we used to explore the woods together. We'd sometimes walked through foggy trails, much like the trail I was on. I'd follow his auburn rain jacket—the only thing visible in the fog. He would shout, "Onward through the fog! Roar!" and I repeated, "Roar!" as we marched through. When the fog lifted, we'd find ourselves in a green meadow chasing cabbage white butterflies, jumping through little streams, counting early-spring wildflowers. Mom always kept us well-prepared: a red plaid thermos of ice tea, plenty of deviled egg sandwiches, and tangerines. Takuya always peeled my tangerines before he touched his. I'd waited for him to be ready. "On your mark," he said when he prepared his fruit. "Ready —" then, we started eating at once, my jaw hurt from giggling while chewing. The Takuya of my memories — walking with a carefree stride, shouting, and laughing in the spring breeze — didn't seem to fit in a bleak office where a single smile could lose your credibility as a stiff accountant.

After my long slogging climb on switchbacks, the clouds thinned and parted. I was pretty much spent when I spotted the sign for Karamatsu Dake Hut, which Takuya used as his base. My watch showed it was after 6:30 pm; the summer afternoon was deepening.

"Ah! You made it, Misako!" Takuya walked down from the slope, with an ear-to-ear smile, and wearing an auburn jacket over a gray flannel shirt. He looked like that bouncy young boy again. I fought back my tears of relief and smiled, yelling, "Hey!"

He grabbed my backpack and guided me to the table he'd set it up. The majestic, rugged peaks of Northern Japanese Alps poked out above a sea of clouds, looking like an archipelago. I lost my words, and he was nodding proudly.

"I thought you might have an overnight at the bottom. How's it going?" he asked.

I was going to say "fine," but my mouth spewed, "I got divorced."

He paused for a moment with widened eyes and said, "Do

you wanna talk about it?"

I shook my head.

"Okay. Hey, you became free again!" He patted my head like I was a kid, which made me smile.

He was right; being free was something I always cherished. Akiko had said the same thing: I became free. All the expectations from the in-laws, extended family, and society created an invisible cage. I tried hard to live within those boundaries, even though I often felt suffocating. Now the cage was gone, but the idea of freedom had become foreign to me.

"You must be hungry, as you always were." He chuckled, carrying his portable stove over to the table. As he turned the knob, skinny blue flames lit an aluminum pan filled with water. He put in a couple of curry pouches.

"It might take a few minutes," he said. "The water up here is melted snow, so . . ."

I took out the *oyaki* from my backpack and handed it to him. The wrapper had puffed up into a balloon at the high elevation.

"Oh, hey, you remembered my favorite. Thanks, this will be a perfect appetizer."

"They are cold, though."

"Nah, everything tastes good up here." He popped it open, picked one, and smiled. The sun was setting behind the mountains — coral orange rays ran through a sea of clouds.

"It's so close to the sky here," he said, "I can feel the earth's rotation. It's not that the sun is setting; we are brought to the other side, you know?"

As we admired the alpenglow, the last portion of the sun hit the rugged mountain tops. They looked like embers, hot but fading.

"Sometimes, you need a distance to see things clearly." Takuya seemed to be talking to himself. "Look." He pointed to the hillside. Although the hut had basic facilities to stay overnight, many hikers opted for tent camping on the slope. Each tent was now lit from within; they formed a twinkling constellation. Takuya lit two lanterns of his own. As he poured the food over each plate, trapped steam escaped from the pouch and blended into the dark.

"Smells good," I said.

"These are instant curry, though." He handed me a plate.

"Nah, everything tastes good up here," I mimicked him. He tapped my nose with the spoon, and we both laughed.

***

I wanted to feel the earth's rotation, so I woke up before dawn. I waited in the darkness as the indigo slowly lightened. Then, the celestial world began to appear around me in breathless silence. The mountain peaks started changing colors, the many shades of red turning to gold as we were moved forward into the sunlight. I did feel that way; I was brought forward with the mountains. I had forgotten how much I loved watching the sunrise. There hadn't been enough time when I was married, but even now, I remained in a rut.

"Want some coffee?" Takuya came out of the hut with his camping gadgets and spread them on the table.

"You look happier and healthier now," I said.

He nodded, counted the coffee scoops, poured them into the percolator, and lit the burner.

"Was it too much work at the accounting firm?" I asked.

"Oh, no. Gosh, no. Compared to what I'm doing now, it was nothing. But I like it here a hundred times more. Wait, a thousand, or ten thousand times? I forgot how to count already!" He reached for some quartz stones on the table. Turned in his hand, they glimmered, afire.

"Wow, are these for real?" I gasped.

"That's what I said when I found them on the ridge. I love being in the mountains. Finding something unexpected like these makes me more appreciative — keeps me humble." He admired the rocks in his hands and gave them to me. He'd always loved exploring the woods and trekking the beautiful backcountry. "I should have changed the job much sooner, you know?"

The percolator started spurting, releasing a strong roasted coffee aroma into the morning air.

"I didn't disrespect the accounting job, but it wasn't for me. I knew it from day one. The worst part was that I hated myself for doing it day after day."

"I had no idea you had been suffering that long."

"I hid it well. I got a job at a well-known firm: money was good, people were also good. Who am I to complain, right?" He checked our coffee.

"The tricky thing is, there are often some good parts in any bad situation. If you keep balancing pros and cons without knowing who you want to become, the list goes on forever. You have to make it up in your heart what kind of life you want to lead. If you don't, you grow numb to your feelings. And then, it gets easier resting on what had been familiar in your life. Not a good thing to let it happen." He poured the coffee and passed me one in a blue enamel mug.

"When my old friend Masashi offered me a job working in the wilderness, I panicked and clung onto what was familiar. And then . . . you know the rest." He mimed drinking. I nodded.

"Deep down, I feared experiencing poverty again. So, I prioritized earning money, not paying attention to myself." He looked at me.

"I learned it the hard way, so I hope you won't have to. Choose something you can grow into, instead of focusing on what you can get," he said.

"Do you think you found the right path for you?"

"Yeah, the sky, the woods, the mountains; I'm in my element! Plus, I love the idea that someone enjoys the trail without knowing I maintain it. Telling people what to do in the office wasn't my thing. I'm a behind the scenes guy," he said.

"How did you make up your mind?" I asked.

"Trial and error. I think that's the only way to find it out. Even though it's time-consuming, it's worth it." He smiled.

"I must warn you, Misako," he said. "When you start trying different things, many will ask you, 'what the heck are you thinking?' but you don't have to explain yourself. You need to keep focusing on your stuff."

I tilted my head. "Did it happen to you?" I was curious.

"All the time! They were worried, so I couldn't just ignore them, right? But if I tried to reassure them, I would have lost my momentum, and I couldn't afford it."

"How did you answer them?" I asked.

"I said, 'thank you for caring,' and changed the subject. I can be sly." He laughed. "Being happy and looking happy are two completely different things. Happiness can come in many forms, and choosing your own is up to you. You don't have to convince anyone or ask them to understand your choices. Everyone has different tastes. I also kept saying this to myself: What others think of me is none of *my* business."

"None of 'my' business?" I asked.

"Oh, yeah. People's opinions are based on who they are, not who I am. Sure, it's nice if people like my ideas, but it's up to them, right? I needed to concentrate on *my* stuff." He poured another cup for us both.

"So, what's your next step?" He asked.

I looked into my lap and sighed. "I think the head of HR wants to get rid of me."

"Get rid of my Misako? Nonsense!" He raised his arms and then looked at me.

"But do you want to stay at the company?"

"That, I don't know. I'm so disappointed in myself for not knowing that," I said, putting my chin on my hands on the table.

"Well, then, this is the perfect time to learn about yourself, isn't it?"

I looked at him, with my chin still resting on my hands.

"Start thinking about it. What excites you? Remember yourself? Before you got blinded by love?" He winked at the word "love."

"I don't remember. It's been like a long rollercoaster ride," I said.

"If you can't think of anything, here's an idea. Start with what makes you want to say 'yuck.' Trust me, that will do the trick."

"Yuck?" I chuckled.

"Yeah, your mind could be dormant right now. You were busy dealing with that bastard and fitting into a tight society and all. When it's too much, we shut down our desires, and it's only natural. Complaining is generally easier, right? Use it as a warm-up."

"A warm-up," I said.

"Yes. Don't stop there, though. Start thinking of what would be better, and what you can do about it. And then, try everything that catches your attention. Do something. You'll thank yourself later."

"Thank . . . myself?"

"Yeah, why not! I'll tell you the scariest story you'll ever hear. Imagine you're . . . say, you're 125 years old," he said with a mischievous smile.

"Well, that's scary." I rolled my eyes.

"Oh, it gets scarier. Imagine you're on your deathbed, in a hospital room. You think about the dreams you didn't pursue, the trips you didn't take, and the books you didn't write.

You wanted to do them all, but there were always naysayers, and you folded. You did everything you were supposed to do, expected to do, so you should be happy, but you're not. It's too late now, so you're sobbing. An old lady in the next bed asks you if you're okay. She has scars on her face, arms, everywhere, so you ask what happened to her. 'Oh, what a wonderful life I've had,' she answers. 'These scars are my reminders that I lived my life, so I'm proud of having them. Some things went wrong, but I did my best, so no regrets.' You say, 'Wow, that's great. I wish I were like you,' and the woman's eyes meet yours. She has a sparkle in her eyes, just like you used to. 'Don't you recognize me?' she says and reaches out. 'I've tried everything you thought but didn't do. I'm the person you could have been, Misako,' She disappears into flower petals, and there you are, alone in the room."

"Oh, no! Gosh, yikes, I will have a nightmare, oh, goodness!" I screamed, leaped up from the chair, and jumped around as if to shake off the scary image. Takuya laughed, put a frying pan on the stove, added some butter and bread in the pan.

"I know, right? You and I both know that whatever we do, there are pains, even if we are playing it safe. The question is that do you want to meet the person you could have been on the last day of your life, or do you want to *be* that person? It's your life. Decide for yourself what's important to you. Life's short. We can't take it for granted," he said. And he was right.

For our mother and Takuya's father, it was extra short. His father was killed in an accident at work when Takuya was a toddler. In our parents' era, practicing levirate marriage was still accepted. Mom was requested to become the wife of her brother-in-law. She refused. Her parents tried to convince her to take the offer, but again she said no, so the family kicked her out, waiting for her to come back and ask for forgiveness. Instead, she started a business altering dresses, borrowing her friend's sewing machine and a small corner of her house. Then she bought a lunch cart. It got popular, and she became independent. My dad fell in love with her at the lunch cart, and that was his favorite story.

"Life isn't always easy, but that's the fun part." It was one of Mom's favorite sayings. She was always the powerhouse of the family, until her last breath.

Life is short—I nodded. Takuya handed me a plate with crunchy, buttery bread and runny eggs. Everything was perfect. I gave him a thumbs up. He always did wonders with breakfast, and I was glad that I'd hiked up with those cumbersome eggs.

"If you lost everything, you could always hike up the mountains. I'll be working somewhere in this area, anyway."

"That's very helpful!" We both laughed, since the area was one of the largest, deepest mountain ranges in Japan, and his assignment covered an extensive area.

"It's your life, and it's your decision. Decide for yourself what's important to you. Take some time. It's worth it. Whatever you choose, go all out, Misako. You're stronger than you think. We all are. Be *genki*."

The sun hit the snow, contrasting with the deep blue sky, and I nodded to my brother.

Sushi-packed Train

After I came back from the mountain, I tried whatever caught my eye. Business and marketing classes, pottery, photography, sales training, speed reading courses. I was an omnivore, but nothing 'clicked.' All these diversions provided enjoyable moments, but the fun faded quickly. Always by the next morning, the excitement was over, and I found myself exhausted, even regretting the fact that I hadn't gotten enough sleep to tackle the train commute.

Commuting by train to a big city, especially during the morning rush hour, would take a certain amount of endurance. Almost every morning, when the packed train arrived, it seemed impossible to fit inside. Commuters would take a last deep breath, and a specialist wearing white gloves would cram us into the train. We called it a "sushi packed train" —just like sushi rice, we would lose our individuality and become one chunk. Once the doors closed, no one would say a word. Nothing more than a grunt or moan. I'd hear the door closing and know I was rice—an uncountable noun.

With nothing else to do, I'd let my mind drift away to stay sane.

"Follow the proven path. Be realistic now. You can thank me later." My high school teacher's baritone voice had popped up in my mind. He was telling me to take home economics for extracurricular credit to learn how to be a good wife. I remember saying no. Also, I'd probably said something crazy that made him upset, because the next thing I remember, he was shouting in my face. "You can't try anything just because you like it. It's too childish. Grow up, will you?" He repeated because I didn't say yes. "GROW UP!" His glare and red face were hard to forget. Yet, I couldn't remember the essential part.

I'd told him my plans — my desire — before he shouted at me. What *had* my goal been back then? I knew he'd tried to teach me the structure of Japanese society — that anyone too different runs the risk of being selfish. We have a saying, "The nail that sticks out should be hammered down," instead of, "The squeaky wheel gets the grease," in the western culture. I knew I was expected to do the same as others.

"Being obedient is a survival skill for a girl like you — one without talent or family money. Just be obedient like the others, won't you?"

How I'd loathed those words. Then, I felt something on my thigh. *Not again,* I thought. It was all too familiar, *chikan. Chikan* is a man who gropes women on a packed train, and it was widespread in the metropolitan area. I didn't even remember how many times those bottom dwellers ruined my day.

Of course, I'd assumed it was an accident or someone's bag touched the back of my thigh. However, as I turned my body, the thing would follow my leg, even start moving up. *Chikan* knew no one could move in the sushi-packed train, and it was hard to report. I was wearing high heels for fighting off *chikan*, so I could stub his toes with all my rage. If he was committing the crime, he wouldn't make a noise, I'd learned over the years.

So I did. The guy didn't say a thing and stopped touching me. Then, I thought, *how on earth am I enduring this for years and years? Wouldn't this be the most obedient act or what?*

I spewed, "Yuck." Takuya was right. Thinking of something that made me say, "Yuck" was a good warm-up; I felt my senses were coming back. I needed to do something more than attending those short courses. I needed a bigger change, and I knew it deep down.

When the train spat us out in the business district station, we transformed back into individuals. We spread out on the platform and walked toward the exits without a word as if we were marching to the same drumbeat. No one was supposed to disturb the pace, but I missed a step on the stairs. Instinctively, I reached for a shoulder in front of me, but the owner of the shoulder also instinctively swayed. I fell onto the stairs, upside-down. Thanks to my former gymnastic training, I didn't twist my wrist or hit my head too hard, but it required significant arm strength to get up from the position, and I struggled. Even though my fall was hard to ignore, others just kept going. See No Evil. Japanese are well known for their politeness and kindness. Still, after being stuck on a train for thirty minutes or more, we lose our humanity. In the business district train station, we were like wildlife migrating across the African plains, driven by instinct and necessity. I was a fallen wildebeest on the Serengeti plains—left behind to perish if I couldn't get up by myself.

After several embarrassing attempts, I managed to pull myself up through the stream of traffic, but I was in everyone's way. A man said, "Chop-chop!" as he shouldered in. Someone pushed me, and another clucked his tongue as I was losing my balance. Like a ball in a pinball game, I was helplessly pushed to the wall, where I bumped into another man, who elbowed me. It was just like my life, being pushed in every direction . . . aimlessly.

It became clear that if I didn't decide my direction now, I'd continue to be pushed around. *No, not like that, NO!* I sped to the exit and hurried through the ticket gates. I squinted my eyes in the sun as I stepped outside. It was one of those perfect early autumn days you often see in movies. The sky was clear, deep, and serene, and there were a few cold threads in the air.

I left the crowd and headed to Yamashita Park, a narrow seaside commons that extends along the waterfront of Yokohama Harbor. It had been a while since I last visited the park, even though it was less than a mile from the station. I wanted to see the Hikawa Maru, a retired ocean liner converted into a floating museum. Her maiden voyage had been from Japan to Seattle, Washington, in 1930.

Then, she'd crossed the Pacific Ocean more than two-hundred-fifty times, and it's estimated that she carried around twenty-five thousand passengers in her thirty years of service. She'd also served as a hospital ship during WWII. I walked into the park, and there she was, basking in the autumn sun, resting on the dark blue water. I leaned on the fence and admired her, letting the harbor winds comb my hair.

"Bridge across the Pacific." The phrase came into my mind. It was coined by Inazo Nitobe, the author of *Bushido: The Soul of Japan* in 1899.[4] He wrote it in English instead of his mother tongue. He was also the first exchange professor between Japan and the U.S.

"1899 . . ." I mumbled. How crazy it must have seemed from everyone else's perspective. At the same time, how exciting it must have been for him, sailing into the unknown. I imagined Mr. Nitobe on the deck, looking beyond the horizon.

What if I chuck it all and start traveling in a different country? The notion rose like a mighty swell. I'd forgotten the feeling of energy surging deep inside myself. To experience the world, stand on the soil, breathe the air where I'd never even imagined — *wouldn't it be the adventure of a lifetime?* I gasped as a frisson — what we call it a samurai shiver — ran through me. It stung a little.

A group of women walked past me with a guidebook, and one of them asked me to take a photo of them. I took a few shots and handed back the camera.

"Yokohama is such a beautiful city," she said with a big smile.

"I think so, too. Enjoy Yokohama," I replied.

A beautiful city, indeed, I thought. I had friends, a stable job, a cozy apartment — I'd built my life here.

"I can't leave Yokohama. It was just a crazy idea. It's too crazy, right?" I look out on the Hikawa Maru in the morning sun, as if she might reply.

The bright morning reminded me of seeing off Nanami.

She'd left for Paris before I graduated high school. The staff from the bakery and I were at Narita International Airport to see her off. No one from her family was there, but we knew Nanami was a private person, so we didn't ask about it. She was wearing an indigo tweed jacket. Inside was a crisp white shirt and jeans, and her maroon carry-on bag made her version of the Tricolore. She went into the security check, turned around, and waved one last time. The sun filled the departure lobby with champagne rays, but Nanami's smile was brighter. Later, she sent me an email. Her life in Paris was full of challenges, and she enjoyed every single one of them. She landed her dream job. "If it excites you and scares you at the same time, it probably means you should do it," her email said.

I mumbled what Takuya had told me. "It's your life. Decide for yourself what's important to you."

Strings of various national flags were dancing in the wind on the Hikawamaru's upper deck, and a chain stretched into the water. She looked ready to sail away at any moment.

Chapter 3

N for Navigate Through Changes

"Change your opinions, keep to your principles;
change your leaves, keep intact your roots."

—Victor Hugo

Pago Pago, American Samoa

Hot, humid, and suffocating, a blast of tropical air flooded the airplane, colliding with that of the over-chilled cabin as the flight attendants opened the door. The tides of the two were palpable. Had the air-conditioning been a tad more robust, those air masses could have formed rain clouds.

My flight from Hawaii landed at Pago Pago International Airport, American Samoa, on-time— 9:30 p.m. The airplane rolled up to the airport apron in a downpour. The stairs didn't have a roof, so I gripped the wet railing and carefully made my way down. I'd never experienced such big raindrops. I hunched over my carry-on bag, trying to protect my PC. I followed people heading to the airport building, probably a hundred yards away. Most of them were Samoans returning home, and they didn't seem to be bothered by walking in the rain. I noticed that everyone else was wearing sandals, and there was a reason for it. My favorite walking shoes became a pair of mini-buckets. Splash, splosh, splash, splosh. Each step sounded like a creature crawling out of the water. I could write a funny article on this. I giggled. I'd made myself a travel writer during this solo trip, even getting a couple slots in magazines.

It was a long journey. At the moment, I was 6,400 miles away from my home country, and over two years had passed since I left Japan with my two suitcases. I'd meandered through New Zealand, Australia, South Korea, and Hawaii. I walked a lot, including strolling through botanical gardens, but no one ever walked as slow as these people around me. My mind was slipping through the crisp winter mornings in Auckland harbor. The scorching Australian outback with its high contrast shadows on blood-red soil. The bustling city of Seoul. The sweet scent trade winds in Honolulu.

"Ick!" I jumped with a small scream. I kicked something heavy, cold, and eerily soft—a fat toad. There were many of them waddling on the ground. Some had already been kicked away and were showing their bellies; others were trying to pass the sluggish human procession.

William Somerset Maugham chose this island for the stage of his short novel, Rain. In the story, the incessant tropical rain foreshadowed travelers' tragedy. It's going to be interesting. I smiled.

Morning on the Tropical Island

I woke up to a vaguely familiar, motel-looking apartment with popcorn-colored ceilings, dingy lace curtains, and faded sheets. My suitcases were still in the corner of the room, with airline tags on them. I'd arrived late the night before, and it hadn't yet sunk in that American Samoa was my new home.

I got off to the linoleum tile floor, dug out a few items, and went to the bathroom. The wall was covered in a heavy coat of white paint, and natural light was coming in from the frosted glass window. I pulled back the cream shower curtain. It was a simple, white-tiled shower stall with a shower arm poking out from the wall, looking down on me. There was no showerhead. Is this the way they take a shower? I was unsure but entered and twisted the taps. Lukewarm water gushed out and pounded my forehead with incredible force. In my home country, there is a Shinto ritual called takigyo, in which a monk goes under a waterfall to meditate and purify his soul — to strengthen his spirit. I had never thought I'd experience it in my life. Especially on a tropical island. Gasping, I felt along the wall until my fingers found the faucets, and I adjusted the water pressure.

After repositioning myself, it was soothing. I let the water hit the backside of my neck and cascade down my body, washing away the long flight's grogginess.

"So, this is going to be my base for a while." Refreshed, I started checking the apartment. Each window was filled with lush jungle. It looked like the rain had let up before I awoke. Morning dew sparkled on the leaves. On the wall, there were a few geckos, along with a vine sneaking into the room from the air conditioning unit. Everything was telling me that I'd traveled far away from my home country. I started humming "Beyond the Sea" and twirled into the kitchen.

The kitchen was adequate. An oven, a fridge, an old microwave oven, and a coffeemaker sat on the white-tiled counter. A simple set of silverware was in the drawer, including a spatula, knives, and a ladle. *Not bad. Not bad at all*, I thought and banged the counter like a drum. Still humming, I opened the cabinet.

Thud. Something fell onto the floor. Something long, wiggling, and fast. It was a giant centipede—bigger than any I'd ever imagined. I leaped backward, grabbed the dish detergent bottle, and spewed it over the thing. It reared up, with cords of green liquid dangling from its body. No longer a creature, it looked like a monster. I screamed and threw a pile of newspapers on the beast, then jumped, stomped, twisted, and squashed it. My mind was wholly consumed by fear, far from the fleeting Zen shower.

"Is everything okay, new neighbor?" A gray-haired man with a tired-looking T-shirt stared in through the window.

"Hi, yeah . . . good morning, sorry for the noise. I just killed a centipede," I replied, huffing.

"Oh, you killed it, huh? They eat each other, so some will come to eat the dead one," he laughed, but I couldn't join in. The man introduced himself as Sione and explained that I should have boiled some water and poured it over the centipede. "If you do that," Sione continued, "The centipede would become rubbery, emitting no scent. That's the safest way. Clever, huh?" He tapped his temple.

I wasn't sure if anyone would have time to boil water with a giant centipede running toward them, but I nodded.

Now I had an urgent mission. I needed to get rid of the dead centipede before the scent would attract others, so I dashed outside and gasped. There it was, the Pacific Ocean sparkling under the morning sun. Waves broke in the distance. The emerald water shimmered past the shallow reef, gently lapping a coral beach. Having arrived late in the night, I'd only seen the haze of rain lit by streetlights, but the apartment was on a small hill, so I could see the ocean from the front door. I almost forgot that I still had the dead creature wrapped in a newspaper, so I hurried to the jungle and threw it as far as I could. After flapping the newspaper until it ripped, I looked up at the tropical trees. There were bananas, papayas, and palm groves. Behind them stood a thicker jungle, climbing up the blue sky. A magnificent white bird was soaring in front of the cliff, turning in the up flow. I squinted my eyes when the bird's long tail reflected in the sun.

"You didn't get bitten, did you?" Sione asked me. I shook my head, and he said, "Do you see those plants there? They help when centipedes get you." He smiled. 'When' not 'if.' I'd later learn his word choice was all too accurate.

Unwritten Rules

The next mission was to get groceries . . . and a showerhead. Sione said, "Go to KS-Mart. It's on the other side of the island, but they've got everything. If they don't have it, you wouldn't need it here." There was one main road, a two-way that went from one end of the island to the other, and the speed limit was twenty-five mph, with no traffic signals. According to the map, long stretches followed the coastline, hugged by coral reefs. It looked like a scenic drive.

"Why not?" I said, hopping into the old, white Suzuki Sidekick I'd borrowed. I soon learned that there seemed to be hidden rules everywhere, so I had to pay undivided attention at all times. Some drivers would stop in the middle of traffic to let others in. Some would cut in front of me, then proceed to drive ten mph. Some would start chatting with pedestrians, matching the pace of their stroll. No one went faster than fifteen mph. No one seemed to be bothered by anything. The southeast trade winds blew through the car. I was probably the only one tensed, confused, and gripping the steering wheel.

I made it to KS-Mart, and let out a big sigh, resting my forehead on the steering wheel before going into the store. Inside, it was cold as a refrigerator. Lay's, Pringles, and a hundred other potato chip brands filled the shelves. They did have showerheads. Meanwhile, the produce section was tiny, and a head of iceberg lettuce had the price tag of eleven dollars. Broccoli was on a plastic tray and wrapped tightly, no longer green, also bearing a scary price tag. I ran through the meat section with half-shut eyes, after spotting a frozen pig face. Semi-panicked, I ended up picking up familiar items: bread, eggs, coffee, butter, canned fish, and frozen vegetables. They didn't have fresh milk, and it reminded me that I was on an island in the middle of the Pacific Ocean. I looked back at the isle filled with large taro potatoes, green bananas, and something I'd never cooked before. "Well, one at a time," I mumbled and headed to the cashier.

On the way home, I couldn't help but notice that many houses had graves in their front yards. I'd read about it before. It was their tradition, but witnessing it in person was a blow to

the senses. Most of them were well-tended: painted and deco-
rated with tiles. Some were under the laundry line. Others were
trodden by children. Upon my return, it occurred to me that
there were graves near the apartment as well. That battle with
the colossal centipede had blinded me. Neighbor kids were
playing around the graves, and some were taking a nap. After
seeing so many around, the next-door grave didn't bother me
somehow.

***

Ding, ding, ding, ding. It sounded like a church bell, but the
sound came from the beach. A teenage girl came to my door.
She was wearing a T-shirt and knee-length shorts under a lavalava, a Samoan wrap.

"Hi, new neighbor. It's *sa* time. Mind my staying here?" she
said.

"Not at all, come in," I said. "But what's *sa* time?"

She scooped up her chin to the window as she sat down
on the couch. As I looked outside, the children playing in the
graveyard were running toward home. The wall clock showed
a few minutes to six.

"This bell is your warning to get off the streets," she said.
"*Sa* officially starts with the next bell."

She was very concise. From what I gathered from her words,
it was called *sa* time, and you were supposed to be inside of the
house or sit somewhere that wouldn't bother others.

"So, what should we be doing?" I asked.

"You wait until it's over, or you will be punished." She pointed outside again.

Men wearing matching lavalava stood on the street with their arms crossed, glaring down the road.

"How long are we doing this?" I asked again.

"Till the next bell."

"When is the next bell?"

"Not too long," She laid down on the couch and playing with her long, thick, and glossy dark hair.

I looked outside. The palm trees were swaying, and the sun was getting low, but those men were stationary. About ten minutes or so passed, and the next bell rang. People returned to the street, and kids started playing again. The men took off the lavalavas and joined people, chatting with smiles on their faces.

"Okay, thanks, see you later." She was leaving.

"Do you know where I can see the bell?"

"Everywhere," she said, as if I should have known, and left.

I went to the beach and asked neighbor kids where I could see one. One of them pointed to a rusty oxygen tank hanging from a palm tree by the street. I'd seen them all over the island. Who'd have guessed they were mighty bells?

Palolo, Samoan Cuisine

The golden rays of sunrise defined the horizon, streaming over the shallow water, and setting the hillsides aglow. I loved dawn on the beach. The gentle morning breeze, the jingling sound of broken coral rolled in and out with the tide — everything was dreamy. Aleki, one of my neighbor boys, played his ukulele when the weather was good.

"Morning, Aleki!" I said. He broke into a big smile and ran up to me.

"Hey! Tonight is the night. it's the *palolo* night!" He jumped and hopped around me.

"Um..., what's *palolo*?"

He stopped, widened his brown eyes. "Oh, you don't know *palolo*? That's really, really sad! You know, it's like angel hair pasta. Long and skinny, and it's so tasty!"

"Oh?" His enthusiasm was contagious; I smiled and widened my eyes.

"It only comes to the reef when the moon is right, and it's tonight. If you miss it, the next one will be a whole year away!"

I was trying to imagine angel hair pasta in the shallow reef.

"Some tourists don't like *palolo*, though. Are you brave enough?" Aleki said.

"Oh, yes, I am! Plus, I'm not a tourist, I live here," I said. He smiled and said he was going to have his sisters wake me up after midnight.

After he left, I looked out on the water and talked to myself. "Whatever it is, it can't be too bad for a sushi-eater like me . . ."

I managed to get up before the neighbor girls broke the glass door with their banging.

"It's time! It's time! Hurry, hurry, hurry!" I was dragged out of the apartment as I opened the door, wearing pajamas.

A girl set my flip flops in front of me, and I slipped my feet into them. Two others took my hands, one pushed my back, and the rest followed, cheering and giggling. We went down the driveway, across the street, and proceeded along the moonlit beach, engulfed in the shadows of coconut trees.

All the neighbors were already in the water, in their regular clothes.

"Hey, you made it!" "Hurry, it's started!" Some shouted, and the loudest voice came from Taimane, the Ukulele boy, Aleki, and his sisters' mother: "Come, come here!"

I ventured in, up to my waist. The water was warm, and the reflection of the moon was swaying along with the gentle current. When I reached Taimane, she gave me a sieve. She had a pasta strainer in her hand and a bucket on her other side. Everybody in the water had a sieve, along with cheesecloth or filter of some sort—even lace curtains and tablecloths. All of them looked excited. Taimane said, "Scoop the surface. *Palolo* will come into your sieve, so put them in my bucket. Just like this." She showed me the motion. I nodded, scooped the moonlit water as demonstrated, and with one scoop, the sieve became heavy. I caught my first *palolo*, so I looked at them.

Their diameter *was* comparable to angel hair pasta. Some were long enough to compare to noodles. Some were bluegreen, and some were brown, all of them wriggling away in my sieve. With lack of a kinder euphemism . . . they were a chunk of wiggling worms. I shrieked, put them into the bucket as quickly as possible, and pulled both of my arms on the water to make sure nothing was hanging them.

"I knew you would like it! Beautiful, huh?" Taimane looked happy. And then, she lowered her voice and looked straight into my eyes: "Now, keep scooping. Our time is limited." Aleki once told me that Taimane was a retired Marine, and I sensed it from the fire in her eyes.

As a neighbor brought a torch near me, I got to see more clearly: *Palolo* worms were now thrashing in vast numbers; the water was entirely covered with them. Taimane screamed: "Now, scoop! Keep scooping!" I did . . . without watching the water.

The *palolo* swarm was over when the plump moon was on the west side of the sky. We'd caught a lot of them. Taimane was smiling with her bucket full of *palolo*.

"We're gonna have a feast on the beach, so don't sleep in, okay? See you in the morning!" Taimane put her fist in front of me, so I bumped it with mine. I hurried home to hop into the shower. *Palolo* worms washed down to the shower stall floor, livelier than I would have guessed. When one *palolo* wiggled between my toes, all my senses went into mayhem. I think I may have blacked out for a minute or two, erasing some of those memories to protect myself.

The next thing I remember, I was sitting at the kitchen table in a fresh T-shirt and shorts, thinking: *Should I escape? I have a car. I could drive up to the other side of the island and spend some time there.* It was doable. *I don't have to eat those wiggling worms, now do I?* I grabbed the car keys. However, I did say "yes" to

Aleki when he asked me if I was brave enough. I had to eat *something*: the worms or my own words. *Should I trust my digestive system, or should I admit that I'm not brave enough?* Gentle trade winds and dancing shadows. Swaying coconut trees. All looked so exotic.

"Nah," I said to myself. I started traveling abroad to experience the unknown. I would regret it if I didn't go all the way. I dropped the car keys.

Aleki and other cheerful neighbors woke me up. I slid my toes into my flip flops, still sticky from seawater, and went to the beach. Two long picnic tables with vinyl tablecloths were set out on a grassy knoll before the beach. Taimane and her kids were bringing plastic patio chairs, and neighbors were starting to seat themselves. Aleki and To'o, Aleki's older sister, invited me to sit between them. French baguettes, heaps of butter, and large casseroles were brought to the tables. The smell was heavenly. When they took off the covers, each pan revealed a unique feast: *palolo* fried in butter and onions, *palolo* mixed into omelets, and *palolo* stewed in coconut cream. The blue-greens and browns stood out, shining.

Aleki was fidgeting and almost drooling. So were others. After a prayer, the host, my landlord, proudly declared, "Dig in!" and that's what everyone did, full throttle. To'o served me a big pile of each delicacy with a big smile. I scooped up a corner of the psychedelic omelet, already knowing the experience would make it into another travel article: the scarier, the funnier. So, I closed my eyes and brought a forkful of *palolo* omelet into my mouth. No doubt, it was an acquired taste, and I wasn't ready. Also, it was scratchy. I gulped down the worms without chewing. Aleki, To'o, Taimane, and others said, "Slow down, there's more," and laughed.

"Good, huh?" Aleki put his thumbs-up, and I did the same. It wasn't for the taste but their kindness — and the exotic experience of a lifetime.

Category Five, Cyclone Olaf

After a few months, I was ready to move out from the beach. I checked the local newspaper's classified pages, and I got to look around houses over the island. Most of the houses were constructed with cinderblock walls, louver windows, and a corrugated tin roof. This was fine by me, but there were other problems — problems I'd never encountered before.

"You didn't tell me you're Asian!" One house owner slammed the door in my face. I was stunned, it took me a while to get what had happened. "Shoo! Shoo! No Asian!" Another house owner "shooed" me away. My blood boiled. I'd heard the expression, but my anger was more intense, almost vaporizing my blood. I wasn't aware of the ongoing conflict between some Samoan and Asian communities.

There were many kind people on the island, too. I made a few friends while I was searching for a house, and I ended up renting from one of them. Annie, a gorgeous Samoan mamma of a big family, was working at a local Toyota dealer, and she and her husband became my landlords. The house was nestled in the middle of a foothill, peeking down at Pago Pago harbor, with a couple canneries and mountains behind it. The house had plenty of space and a big kitchen.

"Here, that's my grandma. And that's my grandpa." Annie opened the kitchen door, and there it was: a graveyard right on the property. "Beautiful color," I said, praising the fresh coat of the paint. Annie smiled, "We just repainted a month ago. Nice, huh?" I nodded and smiled back. I moved into the house that weekend.

A plump Samoan lady with a plumeria flower in her hair approached me while I was sweeping the porch. "Hi, new neighbor. Do you need help?"

We introduced each other, and a few hours later, she brought me koko alaisa, Samoan cocoa rice pudding. It was Lia. I didn't know yet, but she and her family would become a big part of my life on the island.

It seemed that the people there were more open to newcomers than some villages. They didn't seem to mind having me.

It was close to downtown, so I could walk to the stores. Sadly, there were many — too many — stray dogs roaming. Most of them only sent warnings, but some would bite on a whim. There was only one hospital on the island, so I followed Lia's advice and carried a stick in my hand and rocks in my pockets. She also taught me how to yell, "Halu!" "Go away!" in Samoan. It was heartbreaking to see and shoo away the strays, but I learned to accept things as they were. I also learned that acceptance doesn't equate to giving up. It simply acknowledges reality and gives us the chance to prepare for our next move.

Accepting reality without giving up wasn't easy, but that was exactly what I wanted to learn: the navigation of changes.

The climate of American Samoa is like that of any tropical rainforest: hot, humid, and rainy throughout the year. That said, December to March was considered the wetter season. It had been almost two whole months of sobbing rainy days and nights. At this point, my very senses were liquid, and nothing seemed to excite me, but February 15th was a bit different. Small, dark clouds were flying fast, and above them were thicker, more ominous thunderheads. Squalls would hammer the island, stop, and return with a vengeance. The wind was whipping the palm trees harder than ever. It must be a big one, coming or going.

I hopped into the car and headed to KS-mart. The road was congested, and so was the store. I'd never thought of checking the weather forecast on the tropical island, but I should have. I remembered an older man walked up to the hill, used a hand speakerphone, and announced something in Samoan language the morning before. It was probably a warning about the cyclone. I found a stack of newspapers at the cashier, and it said that the storm was a category five. Its size was at least fifty times bigger than the island. All the flights had been canceled, it said. I'd missed the chance to get out.

I grabbed some bread, canned tuna, cookies, water, batteries — whatever I could think of — and threw in a pack of KitKats for my emotional well-being. On the way home, the wind was building, and the high tide was pounding the sea walls, spraying the traffic. Across the rough gray sea, crests were breaking into spindrift, foam blown in streaks. The horizon was gray with weight, and it looked like a wall of clouds moving toward the island. I held the steering wheel tighter, and my breathing was shallow and fast. "Breathe," I said to myself, remembering the mantra: "Stop. Breathe. Channel my inner Samurai." Although I wasn't sure that a Samurai could function in such heat, I made it home.

Just like so many others around, the house consisted of concrete blocks, louver windows, and a metal roof. I called my landlord to see if I needed to do anything in preparation for the cyclone.

"The house has survived many cyclones, so you don't need to do anything," he said, laughing. The line went dead, And I felt alone. In fact, I was alone. I was working with publishers based in Japan; everyone was thousands of miles away. An editor responded to my email, and he was "looking forward" to my cyclone report.

Meanwhile, I was entering a panic. My close friends had already left the island a month ago, saying they were tired of living on a small, rainy island. I did have a significant other in my life, but he was working on a fishing vessel. He was sailing somewhere only latitude and longitude could explain, days away from any land.

I packed my PC, bottles of water, and some food in my backpack. Even with all the windows closed, the wind whistled through the gaps around the doors, and the curtains were flapping. As the evening progressed, I felt a deep, quiet fear. It was strange because I'd mostly been alone since my mom passed away. I'd experienced plenty of typhoons, blizzards, and earthquakes alone, but this time felt different. "Pull yourself together," I said, gripping my elbows and looking outside. The dark clouds looked like a ceiling pressing down, and the gusts had already leveled the banana patches. I saw something moving through the yard, and it was Lia's family, the sweetest neighbors. I opened the door, and a gust hit my face. I couldn't breathe, and it was even hard to open my eyes. I hurried to let them in.

"So sorry, but if it's okay with you, can we stay here tonight?" Lia was panting and told me that they feared that their house might not hold up. Her husband, Ioasa, had a large duffel bag, and their sons, Lani and Asa, each had a bag too.

"Of course, please do!" I said. As I closed the door, a metallic sound came from the street.

We peeked out the window to see what had caused the noise, and just as we did, a sheet of a corrugated roof smashed onto the street, dragged along, and spun away like a Frisbee.

"Oka! (Oh my God)" Lia brought her shoulders to her ears, and I widened my eyes and nodded, unable to speak. "Oy!" then she said, pointing at the porch. There were two skinny puppies there, shivering. I gulped the air before opening the door, grabbed the puppies, and dashed back into the house. Most likely, they were strays.

"Well, they can stay with us until the storm passes," Lia and

I said it at the same time and chuckled. I put the puppies into a cardboard box with my old T-shirt, and they seemed to be okay with it.

After Lia's family changed into dry clothes, they helped me move the furniture to the safest walls. I brought all the cushions and linens to the middle of the house, away from any windows, and that's where we all settled.

Lia and her husband, Ioasa, were immigrants from Independent Samoa, the island of Savai'i. Both of their sons were strapping. Lani was in high school, and Asa was in junior high. They were hard workers, polite, and caring, just like their parents. I often saw the boys studying under the Samoan lemon tree. Or sweeping the street, cutting grass, shredding coconuts, and tending their small patch of bananas, taro, and breadfruit. Everyone in the family broke into a smile whenever they spotted me, and their smiles brightened my day without fail.

Ioasa brought his radio and translated the weather forecast for me. Mile by mile, the category five cyclone was ripping through the islands without losing power. The wind kept howling, and booming gusts rattled the house from time to time. Heavy rain pounded the windows. At last, the flickering lights gave up, so we lit one of the flashlights. As the warm light lit us, I felt like we were gathered at a campfire.

"What if the water stops like last time?" Asa asked. He said the last cyclone, several years ago, had devastated the island. I'd seen badly damaged and abandoned houses here and there—claw marks from the past cyclones. Lani told me that they'd been forced to go to the waterfall beyond the hill for a week.

"A week without water?" I repeated, and they nodded. Imagining the worst, I put my hand over my mouth.

"Well, try not to let your imagination run wild, huh? If the water stops, we'll deal with it," Ioasa said with a smile.

"He is right about that. We can always give our mind the right direction," Lia said. Ioasa looked at her fondly. She told me about their home island, Savai'i, about 120 miles away. It's the biggest island of the Samoan Islands. Cream-colored beaches contrast with jet-black lava rocks, and people live at a much slower pace than those in American Samoa. There, Samoan culture lives on.

"Do you miss the island?" I asked.

"Oh, yes, of course. It's our root, and this island is, um, different from Savai'i in so many senses. We don't regret our choice, though," she said.

"Home is wherever you decide to make it," Ioasa said.

"When we start doing new things," Ioasa continued, "it's important to remember that we are beginners once again." I nodded, thinking about when I started traveling abroad. As an adult, getting around in my home country was nothing. Once I arrived in a different land, I found myself incompetent. How to use a bus in New Zealand. How to withdraw cash from an ATM in Australia. Learning some basic etiquette on tipping in Hawaii. I didn't know anything and struggled; my ego was bruised.

"Everything gets easier with practice. Struggling means you are trying, not giving up." Ioasa turned his face to his sons. Many leave the island once they finish high school to attend college or find a job in Hawaii or on the U.S. mainland. Wherever they go, it's a different world for the youngsters.

"Finding how little you know outside your world is priceless. That's how you grow, so don't get discouraged. Focus on what you can do about it." Both Lani and Asa were nodding, absorbing wisdom. So was I.

"How about some goodies, yes?" Lia opened a bag of masi Samoa — buttery, flaky coconut cookies. I brought water bottles and paper plates, and the boys helped to serve them to each of us.

"This is fun. It's like Sunday Brunch," Asa said, and Lani continued: "Yeah, except it's nighttime." Lani chuckled.

"That's right. We should eat supper and prepare for bed." Lia opened a bag of bread. I brought peanut butter and grape jelly from the pantry I'd bought earlier at KS-Mart.

"Oh, I almost forgot," said Ioasa, digging into his duffel bag. He picked up a case of canned wahoo fish, handed it to Lea.

"These are for you, as a token of gratitude," Lia held them above her head, the gesture of gift-giving.

"Faafetai lava," I said — the Samoan word for thank you —, "but I'm the really grateful one here. I didn't want to endure the storm alone,"

"Oh, we are glad to know that we are helping each other. You are like our aiga. Aiga means family, you know?" Lia hugged me.

"Well, let's eat!" Ioasa said. We all started making our own sandwiches and ate them.

"Would you like to hear a joke, auntie?" Asa asked me as he was making his second sandwich.

I smiled back and nodded, tickled to be called auntie. It was the first time hearing it.

"Listen to this, auntie." Asa offered me a piece of bread. Have some more . . . sam-ore . . . sam-oah." Asa collapsed with laughter, and Lani continued to the punch line: "Some-more, 'Samoa!'" It was a cliché joke, and I had heard of it more than enough times, but somehow it cracked us up, and we all laughed our heads off.

The rain battered the windows even harder, and something struck the wall with a loud noise, but we were still laughing.

"Well, we prepared for the worst. Bring it on, cyclone!" Lia said, wiping the corner of her eyes, still laughing and panting.

"That's right. Facing it is much easier than being chased by it. Bring it on!" Ioasa said. We all followed, "Bring it on!" We laughed some more.

We lay down with our clothes on, in case the house didn't hold off the storm. The wind was still building, now shaking the house, and horizontal driving rains were buffeting the windows again and again. Something was flapping and banging outside, but the house was full of peaceful snoring. I dimmed the flashlight, away from the others' eyes. The stray puppies were also sleeping in the cardboard box, curled up in a tight fuzzy ball.

When was the last time I was with my family? It was a distant memory, but I had some memories with the same warmth and comfort as tonight. In my PC bag, there was an old photo — the only one that'd survived through the stormiest part of my life: Mom and me. Mom was holding me from behind, and I was leaning on her legs, squinting in my favorite cowboy hat. I was probably four or five years old, in my red cowboy clothes. Mom was in an apron, and her glossy black hair was neatly bound behind her neck. Dad had taken the photo. I could tell from Mom's smile, so relaxed and content. Behind us was a yellow Nissan truck, and patches of blue sky poking through a Kunugi, sawtooth oak tree's bare branches. We had two dogs, an Akita mix named Buffy and a Shiba Inu, Koro. I stopped my thought process — closing the imaginary treasure chest before my memories could reach the part where my family was ripped apart. I closed my eyes.

I woke up to the wild rooster's crowing and sunlight flooding in through the windows.

"It looks like the cyclone has passed," said Lia, sitting up and combing her gorgeous long wavy hair, then made it to a bun.

"It sure did," we both got up and went to the kitchen. There, Lia started making koko Samoa, a local hot chocolate drink. Meanwhile, I prepared the French toast. The scent of chocolate and butter filled the room, waking up Ioasa and the boys.

"We made it through the cyclone," said Ioasa, embracing both sons with a smile.

"We sure did," I replied, noticing they'd moved back my furniture to the original places. We sat at the dining table with a large pile of French toast, and a big pot of koko Samoa. There was something special about sharing food from the same pots and pans — enjoying them together. Ioasa translated the radio news, said there were no casualties so far, even though the cyclone had destroyed many houses.

After breakfast, we fed the puppies and let them go outside. Then we walked to Lia's place. Their Samoan lemon tree had survived, and so had Lia's tiny pineapple patch. The house was flooded, but Ioasa had neatly stacked all of their belongings on the upper shelves. It looked like he'd planned well.

"Look, the storm washed the floor for us," Lia laughed. As I walked back to my place, the neighbor on the other side of the street waved to me. Her house was also flooded, and her toddlers were playing on the wet floor, waddling with glee.

"Our tree was knocked down. We got plenty of these. Want some?" She had two golden papayas in her hands, and she was smiling. I smiled back, "Thank you, but I got plenty, too. Let your kids eat some more . . . sam-oah!"

She burst into laughter, shouting back, "You're finally getting it!" She turned to her husband, saying, "She's getting it!" and her husband cracked a bright smile from behind her, waved at me.

I was an outsider, and they knew I was leaving the island one day. Despite our differences in how we lead our lives, I was starting to learn how much we had in common on a deeper level. I loved the feeling that I was earning a little space for myself in this village.

I had no idea there was a woman in my neighborhood who glared at me every time I walked down the street.

Chapter 4

K for Be Kind to Yourself

*"A good cry can be wonderful sometimes,
and sadness is nothing more than love announced."*

— Neale Donald Walsch

Life with Dogs

"Everything is weird until you get used to it." That's what Lia had told me, and she was right. American Samoa's suffocating humidity, thick air, and huge raindrops became "my normal." From daily *sa* time to having my landlord's ancestor's in my front yard, it all became part of my life. I hung my clothes on the line in the pouring rain and learned to ignore the fruit bats in my papaya tree. I took a dip in the ocean fully dressed, just as others did. Nothing was shocking any longer.

Of course, it didn't make the island paradise, and I was often reminded that I was always an outsider. There was still a conflict between the Samoan and Asian communities going on. My being on a Samoan island seemed to bother some locals. I was yelled at downtown, at the airport, in the parking lot of the bank, "Go away, you stupid Asian!" Some confused "China" with "Asia." "Go back to China!" they'd scream. Some even threw rocks at me when I was on foot downtown. While it made my head burst, I was also protected by Lia's family and most of my neighbors. I was grateful. It was enough for me to ignore occasional incidents. Besides, I wasn't alone any longer. I had my cyclone puppies.

Those puppies were nothing like any dogs I'd ever known. They didn't show any enthusiasm, even when I had food in my hands. Only Lia, her family, and I were able to touch them. Even my boyfriend couldn't. They tolerated my affection, but if I dropped my keys or purse or anything that made noise, they would run away. When I put a leash on them, the brown puppy started shivering uncontrollably, and the white one wet herself. There was no doubt about it: they'd been born as strays. Lia and I gave straight-forward names to the puppies: Ena Ena and Pa'e — Brown, and White in Samoan. They quickly learned the idea of having a name but never came to me when I had their leashes in my hand.

Ena, short for Ena Ena, was a shy boy with pendant ears. He loved coconut shells more than anything. Each Saturday morning, someone in the neighborhood would shred coconuts for their Sunday brunch. Ena wouldn't miss fetching a discarded shell, and he would be nibbling, chewing, scraping off coconut meat for hours and hours on my porch. He never learned how to bark like a dog. He was the only dog I'd ever met that had a woodwind instrument.

With her white coat and brown spots, Pa'e was more skittish than Ena. She barked like a dog and loved chasing around jungle fowl. Sometimes Pa'e was chased back by an angry hen, and I learned these birds could fly up high in the air . . . but their control wasn't so good. I remember bright yellow claws pouncing down from the blue sky, followed by a sharp pain in my arms, which covered my face.

Although both puppies were extremely skittish around humans, they brought their wild side when it came to protecting their turf. My puppies gained the neighbors' trust by keeping strays away. Families with toddlers were extra grateful.

Living on such a remote island, I found a niche. My travel articles were getting attention from the Japanese media, and I was invited to a couple of radio and magazine interviews in Japan. Also, a small TV production company wanted to have a meeting with me, so I decided to take a trip to my home country. Lia and her family were happy to feed the puppies.

When the taxi to the airport arrived to pick me up, both Ena and Pa'e ran to the bush as I expected. As the taxi slowly drove down the main street, though, I saw something brown and white moving along. I blinked hard, but it hadn't been my imagination. Ena and Pa'e were following the taxi. They ran under the breadfruit trees, cut along the mangos, and stopped at the first junction. Heads tilted, they sat down, together, growing smaller and smaller.

It was the very first time they'd chased me. *My puppies chased me.*

Hometown Without a Home

Pago Pago International Airport was hot and sticky. The red-eye flight was freezing cold. My transit airport in Honolulu was pleasantly warm. Then, Nippon Airlines' jumbo plane was, again, a giant refrigerator. If I'd been food, I would've lost my flavor by the time I arrived at Narita International Airport. Exhausted as I was, I'd forgotten how neatly the Japanese dress. I was in a ratty T-shirt, faded jeans, and an old pair of walking shoes, stained from constant rain in American Samoa. This was my best outfit.

I hunched over, grabbed my suitcase, and hurried to the shuttle bus bound for Yokohama, where I'd booked a hotel room. I sank into a seat and watched the scenery passing by my window. The bus arrived in Yokohama during the evening commute hour, and there was a crowd of people on the street. I dragged my suitcase to the hotel and checked in. Then, without unpacking, I headed to the city to get decent clothes.

I went down to the mall underneath the station, where I used to go shopping regularly. Most of the shops had changed, but the atmosphere was still the same. I felt an urge to fit in. So I grabbed a couple of simple white shirts, a navy business suit, and a pair of work-pumps in the same color — basically my uniform from back in the company days.

The radio interviews and negotiations with publishers went well, and I was confident about the meeting with the TV production director. His office was in a multi-tenant building in Tokyo. Its hallway felt like a maze. After making a few aimless circles, I found the office. I fixed my shirt and pressed the chime on the entrance counter. A young woman in a beige shirtdress came and bowed. She led me to a meeting room with gray chairs and a long meeting table under rows of fluorescent lights.

"Ah, you made it all the way from . . . where was it?" The TV program producer, Mr. Suzuki, was sitting on the other side of the table. Somewhere in his forties, with jet-black hair, he wore a salmon-pink polo shirt and khakis.

"From American Samoa, and hello, nice to finally meet you, Mr. Suzuki," I replied. Without a word, he pulled out his business card and gave it to his skinny and young assistant, who ran around the meeting table to hand it to me. Mr. Suzuki slurped coffee and started skimming through my notes I'd sent him earlier, mumbling "Blah blah, blah blah," while spinning his pen. His eyeglasses looked greasy. The young girl brought me a cup of coffee with a single-serving cream and a pack of sugar. "Thank you," I said. She bowed without eye contact and left.

"Hmm." He tapped the notes with his pen. "So, you've been dumped by your husband. Escaped from the country eight years ago, and you've been roaming — what, where? NZ, Australia, Hawaii, hmm. You then washed up on the island — the middle of nowhere. Oh, how old are you?" Before I opened my mouth, he continued. "Ah, a Fire-Horse! A cursed woman, a piece of bad luck." He spoke so fast; it made my brain buzz.

"Hmm, the island is exotic enough. The question is, how can I turn this into a program. You know what I mean?" he scratched his head. My brain was still buzzing.

"Hmm," he said and widened his eyes.

"You know what? I've got an idea. Oh, this will do." he pointed at me with his pen.

"Is your boyfriend Samoan?" He asked.

"No, he's a Caucasian."

"Dang! You can't do anything good for the show, can you?" He banged the table. My brain froze.

"Shoot." He leaned on his chair and looked up at the ceiling. "All right, I can still make it work. How about this? You will make a disastrous mistake while we're filming. Embarrass yourself big. I mean, big. Really big, you know?" He made a big circle with his arms.

I wrinkled between my eyebrows, then squeezed out a few words: "Um, uh. I can't predict when I'll make a mistake."

"It's entertainment. It can be scripted. Besides, you've made so many mistakes already, so adding one more shouldn't be too hard."

"Wha—What do you mean?" I narrowed my right eye.

"Come on, don't play coy. Oh, are your parents still in Japan?"

"No, both are gone."

"They lucked out, huh? Oh, Gosh. If you were my daughter—what a tragedy that would be! I'll have to straighten mine up before she becomes a failure like you." He made fists as if he was grabbing his daughter's shoulders and shaking. "Pull yourself together!" he yelled. "Don't be stupid, or you'll end up on some southern island!" With a burst of wheezy laughter, he looked at his assistant. The assistant chuckled. There was a pounding in my ears.

"Anyway, yeah, your mistake. How about breaking a village rule-thing—something to really upset the islanders, without breaking any laws. We don't want to be sued."

"That's—that's a stupid idea." I couldn't hide my irritation.

His smile disappeared, and a cold, threatening look replaced it.

"Hey, I'm giving you an opportunity to be on a TV program. It's a huge opportunity for people like you. Huge! Don't you get it?"

"I live there, and I respect their rules, so —"

"Oh! Gosh, enough! People like to see a gal mess stuff up. *That* gets laughter. *That's* the golden rule here," he scoffed. "Why else would we be interested in you, huh?"

I barely managed to stop myself from trashing the table. "I don't need this," I said at last, then gathered my stuff with shaking hands and left the table.

I heard him shouting at my back. "Hey, you just blew your only chance! There are plenty of girls younger than you, prettier than you, and more cooperative than you!"

I hurried to the elevator and banged the down button again and again. I sprinted to the station and hopped on a train going back to Yokohama. My hands were cold; my mind was racing aimlessly.

Upon arrival, I headed to a waterfront district, Minato-Mirai, to calm myself down. There were still a lot of vacant lots when I was in Japan, so I wanted to see the early cosmos flowers swaying in the breeze from Yokohama port. The area's development had been completed, and it was now a clean, organized city with towering buildings and shopping centers. People were strolling cheerfully, but there were no cosmos flowers in the manicured gardens. The water was pushed further away from the gardens, nothing like it from my memories. As I looked for an information board, it hit me: *I'm a tourist here.*

In Yokohama, the place where I imagined being most at

home, I felt lost instead. I was a stranger in the city I used to know so well. My parents had left the earth, and my good friends had moved on with their lives. I didn't belong here anymore. It was my choice to leave the country and be an outsider, but it hit me hard for the first time.

This was my final evening in Japan, and I had my last meal alone.

The airport shuttle bus glided out from the bottom of the skyscrapers to a colorless late-afternoon highway. There were a few couples and families on the bus, but I appeared to be the only one traveling solo. The bus rolled over bridges, passing cities and peaceful rice fields. Eventually, it arrived at Narita International Airport, ahead of schedule. I went straight to the viewing deck where I could sit quietly, away from the bustling departure floor. Some people were silently looking outside, melancholic music was playing, and the twilight added additional somberness. It had been a similar scene when I was here last time.

I was with Ginji, the kindest person I'd ever dated. We were watching the silhouette of an aircraft taking off and landing in the twilight. I was leaning my head on his shoulder, and he was combing my long hair. We'd been dating for about a year, and it was our last date. He wanted to settle down and have a big family. I had my round-the-world ticket in my hand, and the first destination was Auckland, New Zealand, 5486 miles away.

"Do you have any plans after New Zealand?" he asked, and I shook my head. I didn't have any itinerary. I planned to see as much of the world as possible and grow through my new experiences — that was my only agenda. I bought an open ticket.

We walked to the departure lobby and stopped, looking at each other.

"Thank you for letting me lead my life in my own way," I wanted to say, but I couldn't. I held his hand tighter. He kissed me one last time and blended into the throng.

It felt like it had happened a hundred lifetimes ago. Yet, I remembered his dark blue jacket standing out from the crowd vividly.

As I proceeded to the check-in counter, a young family with four kids, all under ten years old, was at the next counter. The kids were all giggling and chuckling, circling around their parents' legs. It made me think of Ginji and his desire to have a big family.

"Are you traveling alone?" The ticket counter staff asked me.

"I'm traveling solo." The word "alone" sounded like sandpaper to my ears, so I tweaked it. Although I had a boyfriend, he was working on a large fishing vessel and almost always out at sea. I hated to admit my lacking companionship.

The TV producer's wheezy laughter echoed through my head. I felt a tightness between my shoulder blades. *What have I been doing?*

Coming Back to Be an Outsider

After being repeatedly frozen and thawed out in the air and the airports, I was enjoying a balmy night on the island, American Samoa, again. When the taxi from the airport dropped me off at home, Ena and Pa'e came out from the dark jungle, wagging their tails, with their ears gently pulled back.

"Hey, you guys!" A warm feeling rushed through me. I rubbed their heads, and they let me rub them until I dropped the set of keys. The jingling sound startled them, and they ran away to the bush just as they always did. I chuckled. The porch was lit and swept, and there was a paper bag hanging on the door. There was some baked ulu, breadfruit, wrapped in aluminum foil inside, and a note that said: "welcome back." "Aw, Lia, thank you," I said and hugged the note. I was touched by their kindness; also, I was hungry.

I went to the kitchen, reheated the ulu with some butter. As the buttery scent came out from the microwave oven, I could hear my puppies sniffing. Their noses were pressed up at the kitchen window. I gave them some food, and I remembered what Ioasa had said before: "Home is wherever you decide to make it." I then realized I was at home.

In the days that followed, Ena lost his appetite, rapidly weakening. Many stray dogs were suffering from illness, and Ena seemed to be in the same state. The fact that the island didn't have a single vet devastated me. Ena spent most of the time in his favorite box with my old T-shirt, sleeping. When I brought his food and water, he would open his eyes but not his mouth.

"I'm so sorry, Ena. I'm so sorry," I patted his head, and he wagged his tail twice, sometimes licked food and water from my hands. That was how we communicated for a week. On a rainy morning, he didn't wake up. He wasn't even two years old.

Soon after, Pa'e was hit by a blue Toyota Pickup Truck in front of the house on a sultry morning. The truck drove away as if nothing had happened. I jumped out of the house and huddled on the street, clutching her.

"Pa'e!" I screamed, but I saw the light fade from her eyes as I held her in my arms. "No, Pa'e, no! Come on, come on, come back, baby, come back." As I tightly hugged Pa'e, my entire body was shaking, and everything started looking blurry.

"Yo, Asian! Get out of my way!" That was a neighbor woman, sticking out her head from her car, a Toyota Corolla. She was the only person in the village who didn't hesitate to show her hatred toward Asians.

"Yo! I said, get out, you stupid Asian!"

Not now, I thought. I ignored her and repositioned my arms so I could pick Pa'e up from the street.

"Halu!" She yelled. Halu is only used to chase away stray animals. It isn't for other people unless you intend to insult them. A jolt of adrenaline coursed through my body.

"Go away," I spat my hatred.

"Huh?" she sounded a little surprised, as I had never responded to her rudeness. I peeled myself up from the street and repeated a bit louder—maybe a lot louder: "I SAID, GO AWAY! NOW!"

She widened her eyes, put her hand on her mouth, and drove back to her house. I dragged myself to the porch, which Pa'e had cherished her whole life. When I reached her bed at the corner of the porch, the staggering weight of little Pa'e became unbearable; I could hardly breathe.

I felt the porch sag and weight bearing down on my shoulder. I jerked away, and there were two Samoan men standing side by side, looking down at me. Look-alike, in similar faded T-shirts and basketball shorts. They seemed to be surprised to see me with strings of blood seeping down from my dead puppy.

"What do you want?" I said. Being rude was much easier than trying to be civil.

"You made our mom cry. No good." One of them said after the pause. *What is he talking about?* I lowered my eyebrows.

"You yelled at our mom. She came back in tears," the other one added.

"Well, do you know what your mother said —" before I could finish, one of them stepped even closer. I was in his shadow.

"You don't belong here, Asian," he said.

"Why don't you go home, huh?" The other one pointed to the harbor and smirked.

That smirk snapped something inside of me. I stomped the

ground, stepping forward.

"You think you can intimidate me? Ha! Go ahead! Take a swing and see what happens! Come on!" I stretched my neck, showed my cheek to him. "You think you're stronger than me, huh? You have no idea what I've been through! YOU HAVE NO IDEA! NO IDEA AT ALL!" I screamed, and waves of anger swallowed me.

The next thing I remember is Lia putting her arms around me, crying and screaming. "Oh, God, help us, please, please!" I was flailing, trying to escape with all my strength until I felt Lia's big tears rolling down my arms. I stopped struggling in her arms, still panting.

The neighbors were surrounding us, and some were looking at us from the other side of the street. An old guy walked up the hill. He held a high status in the village, someone told me once. He started to talk to the neighbors and the two men. I couldn't hear them well, but Lia held me even tighter. I sensed that she was afraid of what was going to happen next. I glared at the older man, thinking, *Go ahead, if you want to torment me. It should be nothing for you, guys!*

Then, the two men were pushed toward me by a neighbor, and the older man stood between us. He turned to the men and said, "Apologize to the lady. Let your mama take care of herself, huh?"

The two men hesitated at first, but one extended a hand after wiping it on his T-shirt. The other one followed suit. I couldn't understand their words, but Lia said they were apologizing.

I rolled my eyes and shook my head. My adrenaline was still pumping. A neighbor stepped forward and slapped the men's heads, saying, "You two are such mama's boys!"

The sound of "mama's boys" pierced me. *Dang!* I thought, realizing that I couldn't be mad at them for defending their mother. If my mom were still on Earth and came home in tears, I would have leaped to her defense just the same. I let out a long sigh and then shook their hands. Pa'e was still in my arms.

"Your puppy?" One of them asked, and I nodded.

"I'm sorry," they said in unison, each rubbing Pa'e's head gently before leaving.

Lia and her husband Ioasa helped to bury Pa'e, next to Ena, Snowy, Browny, Kiti, Sapi, and many more dogs Lia had helped in the past.

"I'm sorry I lost my head," I said, finally calming down.

"Don't worry. We know you. You were provoked," Ioasa said, patting the grave with his shovel. "And they were wrong. Your home is here," Lia covered the newest grave with some fresh banana leaves. I nodded, and a ball of emotions welled up inside me. I put my hand to my mouth as if I could swallow the ball, which now closed off my throat.

"It's okay. Pa'e is safe now. It's okay to cry. Sadness is a way of expressing love. It's okay to let it out." Lia patted my back, And I nodded.

I dragged myself home and stepped into the shower, stood under the lukewarm water. As I rinsed off the blood and dirt, my hands felt the bumps and scars on my skin. I'd been suffering from rashes for quite some time, and they'd spread across most of my body. The cause was unknown, and none of those anti-itch creams, lotions, or over-the-counter medicines helped. I saw myself in the mirror, shook my head, and put my clothes on.

"How miserable I am." I let it out with a sigh.

"And you should be." My inner critic had been waiting for a moment like this, and it spewed a backlog of hatred.

"You couldn't do anything to save your puppies. You're useless." It knew what words could bleed me dry. My breath was getting shallower.

"Remember what the TV producer said?" I couldn't escape from the inner critic.

"He was right about you. You are a loser. You're hopeless. No one wants you around, and you know it."

What am I doing here? How did I get here? It felt like waves were drawing the sand from beneath my feet, and I lost my balance. I collapsed on the floor and cried. My heart was wound by long, rusty barbed wire, and it tightened up as my blood pumped. I was afraid of this—tears could drain my energy. I'd grow weak and be defeated. My whole life felt like a series of bad choices, and I kept making mistakes that couldn't be reversed.

"I'm SO STUPID," I screamed, rolling onto the bed and curling into a ball. But the pain was far too much.

"You okay?" I thought I heard a gentle voice. I clung to the warmth of the sound and started searching for my memories. The voice was Akiko's. I was on a sidewalk in Yokohama. Satoka and Chizuko were with me too. The image was adding more sounds and colors. Cheerful chatter, festive music, and warm lights pooled onto the sidewalk from a cozy European-style restaurant. It was a lovely evening in Yokohama. The young leaves and summer breeze scent came alive in my aching heart.

Be Your Best Friend

It was our colleague's wedding party. The restaurant was filled with flowers, and everyone was dressed up, feasting, drinking, and celebrating the couple. Akiko was in her mesh-overlay beaded dress, Satoka's was black with peacock-green taffeta, Chizuko's was graphite, and mine was a navy party dress.

"All right, people, picture time!" A photographer started directing people to the center of the room, and the couple was about to cut the cake.

"Now, how about a kiss before the big moment?" the photographer said.

The young couple smiled and looked at each other.

"Kiss the bride!" someone shouted, and it became a chant. "Kiss the bride! Kiss the bride! Kiss the bride!" The bride blushed, chuckled, and looked at her husband. She tilted her head to receive a kiss and closed her eyes. She was radiant. As the couple embraced each other, a storm of camera flashes went off, and the walls and the floor around me started spinning. I felt my heart racing, lost my balance, and tumbled.

"Whoa," Satoka received me before my knees hit the floor.

"Hey, you okay?"

"No," I forced my voice out, but it was a whisper.

"Hang on." She kept me on her side, pressing through the crowd of people. Her long straight hair was swaying in front of me like a shield.

"What happened?" "Oh, gosh, is she okay?" Every time someone asked Satoka, she casually said, "Yeah, that pink cocktail is a killer." She brought me to the bench outside, and I collapsed onto it. I let out a big sigh and buried my face in my palms. Cold sweat trickled down on my neck, and the ground was still spinning.

"You okay?" That was Akiko, "oh, what am I saying? If you were okay, you'd be eating and drinking, duh!" She always knew how to lighten up a situation. Chuckling, I felt my senses slowly coming back, and the ground stayed put.

"Here, have some water. This might help." Chizuko brought a glass of water to me. I peeled my face from my palms, and I saw all my good friends—Chizuko, Akiko, and Satoka were there, looking at me with worried looks.

"Thanks." I took the glass and sipped the water.

"Maybe, just maybe, it was a bit too soon?" Chizuko sat next to me, gently asked. She was right; it hadn't even been a month since my ex-husband left me for another woman. I nodded and sighed.

When the camera flashes blinded my eyes, I slipped into the moment when I was the one receiving a kiss from my husband six years ago. I was in a wedding dress I'd sewn by myself, surrounded by our wedding guests chanting. Then, I came back to the present, my mind screamed: *What happened to us? Didn't we take vows to be together until death do us part? Oh, wait, he meant until he finds a better woman?* So many emotions flooded into my mind at once, and I crumbled into Satoka's arms.

"I thought I could handle it, but I guess I was still hurt and raw inside." I sighed. Then, anger rose.

"Gosh, I'm so stupid. I should have known. Of course, it was too soon. I pretended to be okay, but I made a scene. I might have stained their wedding day. I'm SO STUPID!" I let it out.

"Oh, don't be so harsh on yourself. There's no use in adding extra pain now," Chizuko said.

"Yeah," Akiko added, "you wouldn't scream at me 'SO STU-PID!' if I were the one suffering, would you?" It was so right, yet so funny, the way she said it. We all laughed our heads off. When we started wiping away our tears of laughter, Aki-ko said, "We've seen how you flare up, and we all know you broke a tile in the office bathroom with one kick. You know, that tile hasn't been fixed! Don't use that power for attacking yourself." Akiko continued, "Yeah, pick your battles wisely, like Oda Nobunaga."

"Wha—what?" Oda Nobunaga was a warrior chieftain, the first unifier of Japan during the Warring States period, in the 16th century.

"Hey, that's what you said, Misako!" Akiko exclaimed.

"Yeah, that sounds like Misako. Oh, your love of samurai warriors," Chizuko chuckled.

"Well, what can I say. I admire Oda Nobunaga, you want me to tell you more about him?" I asked.

"Aw, there she goes," Satoka teased me, and we all laughed again.

"Hey, you also said this: 'Be on your own side and treat yourself as a good friend,' something like that. Remember?" Akiko said.

"Did I?" I wasn't sure.

"That sounds like Misako, too," Satoka chuckled.

"I know, right?" Akiko screamed. "She has an unlimited supply of sayings, quotes, and everything, from samurai warriors to Greek philosophers to Brad Pitt," Akiko spoke with big gestures.

"Oh! And you talk about Nobunaga as if you just had lunch with him last week, but he was a samurai in the 16th century! Seriously, Misako, I sometimes wonder. How old are you? How is it physically possible?" This set everyone off again.

"I don't remember," I said through my laughter. "But that's typical of me; I forget what I said when I need it most. Thanks, you guys,"

A gentle breeze blew over the sidewalk, and Satoka brushed her silky hair from her face. "Sometimes, we all need a little help," she said. We nodded to each other.

The breeze shook the window treatment, and I was back in the house on the island, alone. Thousands of miles away, many years later, each of us had moved on to a new phase of our lives . . . but best friends came to the rescue still.

"Be on your own side and treat yourself as a good friend," I had forgotten the phrase for a long time. I was sure that someone had said as much. Not only that, I knew I'd been helped by this advice on more than one occasion. I repeated the phrase one more time, and my mind slipped away from the island to a bleak winter morning, and again, I was a teenager.

Who Said What

The sky was dark gray — so dark that the snowflakes looked pinkish. It was called *botan yuki*, which meant peony snow. Indeed, they look like thousands of peony petals dancing down from the sky, but it's wet snow — the kind that makes you soak and freeze. My teenage mind often thought peony snow was one of nature's cruel tricks, but it was almost perfect for the day. It was the morning of Mom's funeral.

The undertaker, Dad, my brother Takuya, and my junior high school teacher, Mr. Arima, were there. None of Mom or Dad's family came. Maybe it was more of a farewell ceremony than a funeral. The room was cold, and I was shivering, but the undertaker, in his ancient black suit, kept wiping his sweat with a light gray handkerchief. Dad and Takuya started arguing over something. Then, it became a fistfight. *Not again*, I thought. They had been fighting almost all the time since Mom passed away as if fighting was the only thing they *could* do. I was too tired to stop them or even say a word.

"Please! Put yourself together, both of you!" That was my teacher, Mr. Arima, squeezing his skinny body between Dad and Takuya. Mr. Arima was shorter than them both, but Dad crumbled down to his knees and started wailing. Takuya scoffed at Dad and stormed out. The undertaker slouched, circled around Mom's casket, and fixed the fake white flowers on a picture frame that had been knocked askew. Mom was smiling in the picture, a black-and-white print of poor quality. The simple ceremony was soon complete, and we all left for the cremation service. The snow had stopped, but the sky was still gray. A skinny brown cat crossed the wet street and vanished down a dark alley.

While Dad was thanking Mr. Arima, a black Toyota Crown, instead of a funeral service van stopped in front of us. A woman in a black dress and a pearl necklace hopped out. It was the first and last time I met her, but she said she was Mom's younger sister.

"I—I needed to say this." her voice was trembling. A well-dressed man, probably her husband, in the driver's seat, glanced at me. He wrinkled his nose and then turned his face away as if he'd spotted roadkill.

"I told her to leave you losers long ago! You killed my sister!" The woman pointed at us and screamed. Then, she hopped back into the car. The man in the driver's seat threw a cigarette butt from the window before they drove away. Dad collapsed to the ground. The undertaker was trying to console him, but I stood there, doing nothing. I was wondering where my brother went and if he'd ever come back.

It was early February. In a few weeks, the southeast winds would jolt the frozen branches, and green daffodil shoots would pop up from the slushy snow.

"O, wind, if winter comes, can spring be far behind?" How many times had Mom read us those lines, reminding us that winter wouldn't stay forever? It helped me cling to the image of a snowmelt stream running through patches of daffodils. We would bring a lunch pack and have a nice picnic like we used to. Spring would eventually come back, but Mom wouldn't be there to see it ever again.

Did we kill her? Are we the reason Mom can't have another spring? I counted the tears dropping onto my black shoes. One, two, three. After a moment, four and five dropped together.

"Don't let yourself grow weak. Don't cry now, hmm?" I looked up to the voice. It was Mr. Arima, standing next to me.

"Mom never told me about her sister. I didn't know I had an auntie." My breathing was shallow and hiccupped when I tried to inhale.

"I'm sorry." Mr. Arima said. "The thing is, when people are hurt—like really, really hurt—they might think that the only thing they can do is make others feel the same way as they do. You and I might do it, too. I'm not saying that's okay; you'll regret it if you do."

"Listen," he said, and held my shoulders, turning me to face him. "People say things, but that's beyond your control. When someone says terrible things about you, remember this. Be on your side. Treat yourself as a good friend— Be kind. Think about what you would say if this was happening to Kumiko. She was worried about you."

Many kids avoided me because I wasn't fitting in, but Kumiko treated me as her friend.

I nodded, wiping my cheeks with my wrists. I held the tears and clenched my throat to swallow the big lump.

"You got knocked into a different life, but that doesn't mean you're done. Don't cry. You are the one to be strong. You've got this. All right?" I nodded twice. He pulled up his collar and left.

***

"Be on your side. Be kind to yourself. Treat yourself like a good friend." That's what Mr. Arima said, I finally remembered. Good friends provide comfort and care, and they push each other to grow. They don't beat each other down. Being kind to myself was different from giving in to myself. It was a lifesaver float for me, a powerful antidote to my harsh inner critic. It helped me to stop my mind from wallowing in misery, to process my emotions. I'll be then ready to move through pain, and to grow from it. Then I realized—that's how we build our resilience, with a combination of grit and compassion.

"Auntie? Auntie...?" That was Asa, calling me at the door. I wiped my face and bundled my hair into a ponytail.

"Hey, Asa." As I opened the door, I was greeted by his sweet smile and sugary scent.

"Mom said you should eat something sweet." He handed me a bowl full of Samoan *panikeke*, drop doughnut. The dish was warm.

"Sorry to hear about your little Pa'e. I liked her," Asa said.

"Thank you, Asa. Pa'e knew it, and you were so kind to her.

Tell your mom I said thank you." Asa nodded and hurried to his house. I was sure another bowl full of freshly made *panikeke* was waiting for Asa, and he'd come to me before touching his treat.

I brought the *panikeke* to the kitchen table. I looked at the window, mindlessly expecting Ena and Pa'e would start sniffing from outside. When I saw the papaya tree instead of their smiling faces, my heart sank, and I let the tears trickle down my cheeks. The tears felt warm.

"It's okay to cry. Sadness is a way of expressing love. It's okay to let it out," Lia had said, and she was right. This sadness—an overwhelming pain now—couldn't be separated from love.

I knew the pain would stay with me. It wasn't something to get over or forget. I also knew the intensity of pain would eventually subside.However, that was also a sad fact for me at the moment. Lia probably knew as much, and that's why she wanted me to eat something sweet. It was exactly what I needed. I bit into a piece of *panikeke*, and it was as tender and sweet as Lia and her family. They always treated me as their good friend. Maybe more than that: they treated me as their *aiga*—family.

I was getting married, and my immigration status was changing. I was leaving the island soon.

Chapter 5

I for Integrate Who You Are
with How You Live

"Courage is not the towering oak that sees storms come and go; it is the fragile blossom that opens in the snow."

—Alice M. Swaim

New in Town

"Whoa." I yanked my hands out of the tap water. I was at SeaTac airport, the Pacific Northwest, using the bathroom.

"Are you okay?" A lady with gray hair next to me asked.

"Um, yes. I guess I forgot how the tap water can be cold. Thank you," I said.

"Are you visiting from Hawaii or somewhere warm?" she chuckled.

"I'm starting a new life here." It was going to take too long to explain my journey.

"Oh? Welcome to Washington state, then. Be sure to bundle up. The temperature drops very quickly in November." She smiled as she left.

My husband and I got married on the Big Island of Hawaii and visited Washington state. We fell in love with the mountains, lakes, and fjords in the Olympic Peninsula, and ended up buying a piece of property in the woods. Later, we rented a little cabin nearby and decided to move our lives here. The cabin was on a ridge from which we could see a vast conifer forest, layers of foothills, and snow-capped peaks of the Olympic mountains. The mountains sometimes reminded me of the views of Mom's dream house. A nip in the air, the weight of a

winter coat, knitted gloves, thick socks, and crunchy ground —
everything was different from what I had gotten used to in
my life in the southern islands. Once again, I uprooted myself.
Once again, the learning curve would be steep, but I was excited about a fresh start.

The cabin was furnished, which gave us a smooth start. We
celebrated Thanksgiving together at the cabin. I made roasted turkey, stuffing, cranberry sauce, baked sweet potato, green
beans, dinner rolls, and pumpkin pie — everything from scratch,
except for the whipped cream. My husband bought a beautiful
tablecloth and a bouquet of autumn-flowers and a vase for our
dinner table. A little fireplace kept the cabin warm, and outside
the window, a couple of deer were nuzzling each other in the
misty yard.

After Thanksgiving, my husband went back to the fishing
vessel. We traveled to the airport together early in the morning,
and I had a two-hour ride home. I'd only driven on small islands with laid-back drivers, so going sixty on a five-lane inter-
state highway was intimidating. As an entrance to the highway
approached, I had to remind myself: everyone has to start from
somewhere. I gripped the steering wheel, clenching my teeth,
and setting my shoulders. I carefully merged, made my way
into traffic, and sped up to the fastest speed in my life. Our car,
an old Ford Escape, handled with ease on the road.

One hour later, the highway was running through rural ar-
eas, and I found myself enjoying it. I turned off the highway
and took an exit for a small town. There was a decent grocery
store, and it seemed like a good spot for me to stretch and get

something to eat. The light turned green, and I drove under the streetlight. Everything went into slow motion from there: something dirty white was making its way for the driver's side window. I raised my left arm to protect my head, then took a heavy blow. A big truck smashed my door with a dull thud. My car spun and let out a high-pitched metallic screech—it collided with a blue car and flapped its hood. My own vehicle shook, coughed, sunk a bit, and went silent. All the warning lights on the dashboard lit and blacked out at once. Confused, I closed my eyes. *What just happened?* I could only hear my heart drumming.

"Hello! Hello! Can you hear me, miss?" Someone was yelling outside of the car. It sounded like a man, but the window was now a million tiny granular pieces, barely holding together.

"Your door is damaged, so I'm gonna open the other side, okay?" A moment later, chilly air rushed in, and it smelled like snow. The man with a stubbly chin and a blue flannel shirt appeared.

"I called 911. Are you okay?"

"Oh, um, well, I think so." I tried to take a deep breath, but the steering wheel stopped me. It had popped toward me upon impact from the side, and now there was no room left. My left arm was still up, covering my face. I couldn't take it down.

"Are you in pain?" he asked.

"No, but I'm stuck here," I said, trying to wiggle free.

"I know, but you shouldn't try moving now. I don't see any blood on you, but it was an awful crash," he wiped his nose on his sleeve and squinted his eyes at the road ahead, "Help is on the way," he said. I could hear the sirens.

"The truck ran through his red light and T-boned you. Your car was thrown into mine," he said.

"Goodness! Are you okay?"

"Oh, yeah. I'm okay." He wrinkled his nose and nodded, then turned his head.

"Ah, finally. Hang in there, okay?" All the sirens stopped, and he walked away.

"Hey! Hello! We could use some help here!" I heard him shouting, and a few men in uniform came, removed the door. Then, a young paramedic examined my body and checked my blood pressure, asking if I felt any pain or dizziness — .

"No," I said, exhausted.

"Let's get you out of here. Can you just lean on me? Any pain? Good. There you go. Take it slow." She helped me out of the car, someone wrapped me in a blanket, and I sat on the stretcher.

"How do you feel?"

"I'm a bit disoriented and shaky," I said, and she nodded.

"That's good. You're still aware of yourself,"

She checked my eyes, head, the back of my ears, neck, and my torso again.

"Looks like you were lucky." She took off her light-blue rubber gloves and pointed at the intersection. The truck that had hit me was a large cargo truck. It had a massive gash on the front, and the bumper was gone. My car's drivers-side tire was ripped, the fender was buried in, and the door was now gone, revealing the driver's cabin. The backside was still buried in the blue car's front, which bore a crooked KIA logo.

"Promise me you'll call your doctor if you notice anything unusual, even if it seems minor to you. Okay?"

"Yes, ma'am," I said and hopped down from the stretcher, returning the blanket.

An officer came and told me that the truck driver admitted that he was texting and didn't realize he was approaching the intersection until it was too late.

"Texting?" I had to repeat, and he shrugged his shoulders and nodded. The driver of the blue car had seen the truck run the light, and a few pedestrians confirmed. "No one got injured, at least," said the officer, letting out a big sigh.

"Can your family pick you up?" The officer asked, and I told him I was still new in town and alone, but my insurance company would help me out.

"Okay," the officer said and left. I called the insurance company and was greeted by the automated phone menu. After pressing numbers and pound signs and listening to their mind-numbing advertisements, I finally got a representative. She sounded even drier than the recorded greetings and gave me the address of the closest rental car place. I wasn't sure if I wanted to drive right away, but it didn't matter to her. She listed documents I would need for the claim and hung up. A flurry started up, and my nose burned in the frigid air. The next bus to the cabin was about five hours away, and the cabin was about twenty-five miles away. I pulled up my collar and started to walk, as I thought it was better than waiting. A sheriff's car stopped, and an officer with light brown eyes stuck out his head from the window.

"Ma'am, I'm going to the area, and I heard you could use a ride." His big smile and strong jawline reminded me of Takuya, my half-brother, even though the officer wasn't Asian. I got in the car and sunk into the warm seat. My fingers were cold and still shaking, so I struggled to put on the seatbelt. The car glided down the street and entered the empty highway between the woods.

"I heard you are new in town. Mind if I asked where you're from?" The officer asked. "No, not at all," I said and shared a bit of my journey. The day I left Japan with my two suitcases and roaming around wintery New Zealand with hardly any English skills. Then, my outback camping under a blanket of stars in Australia, hiking around in Hawaii, and life in American Samoa — many hellos and many goodbyes, laughter, and also tears.

"It sounds like you're a brave woman," he said.

"Well, I'm a bit afraid of driving right now, so I'm not sure if that's true," I said, looking down at my lap.

"It's only natural. You might still be in shock. It's okay not to be okay from time to time, you know?" The officer glanced at me through the rear-view mirror. "You'll be okay. You are who you are, and it can't be changed by a stupid texting driver. Plus, fear can be good," he said.

I tilted my head, curious to hear what made him, a sheriff, say so.

"People without fear do stupid things, like texting and driving. What was he texting, OMG?" He laughed, and I chuckled to myself.

"Right? So, fear can be good. It prepares you, and that can protect you. Don't let it grow too big here, though." He tapped his temple. "It's like fire, so you've gotta be in charge. Let it work *for* you. Don't let it grow into a wildfire," he said. I nodded as we drove through the dense conifer forest. We got off the highway and arrived at the cabin.

I thanked him as I got out, and he replied, "Take care. I have a sense that you'll be driving soon. Welcome to the area, ma'am."

The flurry was now a blizzard, and grayish-white enveloped the squad car's red taillights. The snow had already covered the roof of the cabin, making it look like a gingerbread house. I got in, lit a fire in the small fireplace, and stared at the flickering flames. I then remembered I was hungry. While I was preparing hot chocolate and some toast for myself, I thought, *this is a beautiful little place to call home.*

New Territory

The officer was right; I started driving again, and it gave me another level of confidence. I decided to do something I'd been avoiding for the longest time: practice public speaking in my adopted language, English. The goal seemed like a pipe dream, but for that very reason, some of my perfectionism wasn't as demanding as usual. That's what I needed the most: a big dream that excited me. Something almost impossible. Then

I found Toastmasters International, a nonprofit organization. Several clubs in the town said, "Anyone could join and practice public speaking." I signed up, got a set of manuals, and realized that speaking skills were learnable. I took a practice stage: my voice trembled, my heart raced, and my hands got cold, but I did speak in front of club members. I was hooked.

At a meeting in June, a club officer announced the upcoming speech contest. Everything sounded like for someone else, and my ears canceled out most of the details. After the meeting had adjourned, I was leaving the meeting room, thinking about my lunch.

"Misako!" It was Veda who'd come to my side. She was my Toastmasters mentor, a petite woman with a big heart. She had curly gray hair, wore thick glasses, and her eyes were warm. Veda was generous with her time.

"You should compete," Veda said.

"Me?" I laughed, but she was looking into my eyes. Veda was never afraid of being silent. I felt I needed to say something.

"Oh, Veda. You *are* joking, right?"

"No, I'm not. I think you'll do well, Misako."

"But, but, there are some requirements, right? I'm still new, so I, I don't think I'm qual . . . qualified," I stammered.

"You're fine. I'll send you the contest manual, so you can check over the details." Off she went down the sunlit hall.

I walked toward my car, which sparkled in the sunshine. The summer breeze combed my hair, and at that moment, I grew excited about the opportunity.

"Nah, what are you thinking?" My inner voice yanked me back to reality, but at the same time, my phone buzzed. It was from Veda with the manual.

"You are qualified," her text said. I heard my inner voice screaming, "DON'T YOU DARE!"

"So?" "Are you in?" "Only if you want. No pressure." The texts from Veda flooded in. Crumbling, under her questioning, I replied: "Yes." Before my brain could catch up with what I just sent, Veda replied, "These are forms for contestants. Could you please fill them out and bring them to the contest?"

I replied, "Thank you, Veda!" with an exclamation mark. *It really is happening,* I thought. Tides of excitement and fear flooded my mind. Both were intense. My friend Nanami once told me, "If you're scared and excited at the same time, that's something you should do." Recalling these words, I filled out the form and started to prepare.

Having Veda on board, I also asked Joe, another Toastmaster mentor, to help me practice. Joe was a local business owner and had the right communication skills I wanted to acquire. He helped me define my questions and provided abundant examples and answers. "Think of me like a grocery store," Joe always said. "I'll share everything I can offer, but you are the one to decide what will work for your speech. It's your speech, so pick for yourself." This became one of my favorite phrases.

I revised my script multiple times, pulled out *some* of my hair, went to the park to practice in the early morning, got barked at by someone's dog . . . but still, I was fully determined. Both Veda and Joe supported my practice, and I didn't want to let them down.

To everyone's surprise, especially my own, I won through the first two rounds of the contest. The third stage of the competition was held on a sunny summer Saturday.

The organizer gathered the contestants, gave us a short orientation, and we drew a speech order. I picked the last speaker's spot. Terrified and thrilled, I went back to the main room.

"Hey, Misako!" Some of my club members were there. Veda couldn't make it, but Joe was smiling with them. I ran to him.

"How do you feel?" he asked me.

"I'm excited and scared at the same time, and, and, I don't know what am I doing here!" I said in one breath.

"Hey, hey, . . . *breathe*," Joe said. "You can take a breath, right?"

I took a deep one and slowly exhaled.

"Good. If you can breathe, you can deliver your speech. You practiced well. All right?"

I nodded and sat down near my club members. We watched other contestants delivering their polished, well-rehearsed speeches, and each received a big applause. I was intimidated, and I started thinking it was presumptuous of me sitting there as a contestant. The emcee called my name, inviting me to the stage. I stood up and fixed my shirt, panic-stricken. My ponytail felt too tight—as if someone was pulling on it—and the words of discouragement wouldn't relent. *What was I thinking? This was a mistake. It's not too late to forfeit the competition, and, and* – Trembling, I took a step forward.

"Hey!"

I turned to the voice, and it was Joe, looking straight at me.

"We believe in you," he said with a smile. There were familiar faces around him, cheering me up. I nodded and smiled back at them and headed to the stage. Something was lurking behind the cheerful crowds, I felt, but I pushed myself onto the stage. I took a deep breath and saw the audience again. No one was glaring at me, but the fear persisted. "Bring it on," I said to myself, and dove into the story I wanted to share with my friends.

The next thing I remember is a thunder of applause, and it was for me. I got second place, a silver trophy was placed in my hands, and everyone was cheering. I was looking for a place to return the trophy, but the emcee laughed, "That's too funny. It's yours, Misako. You've earned it."

I looked at the trophy in my hands. It reflected the sunlight, and it hurt my eyes. *I don't deserve this*, I thought.

Old Scar

"I heard that you represented the club well, Misako. Congratulations," Veda said, fixing her glasses. We were headed to another Toastmasters meeting in an office building. The fullness of summer passed through the big windows.

"Thank you for your help, Veda. It was a team achievement."

"You really could be speaking professionally," Veda said.

"Oh, Veda. I don't have anything useful to say."

"That's not true. You do. We all do." Veda looked at her phone.

"I'm sending you some links that might be helpful. I do think you have potential. Put some effort into it," Veda said, smiling. As she turned, her water bottle caught the sunlight, cast a prism on the wall.

After the meeting, I clicked every link she gave me and came across Darren LaCroix, his 2001 Toastmasters International winning speech. I watched it, and my jaw dropped. I watched it again. And again. I couldn't "watch through" Darren's video. After many replays, I shook my head. *Wow*, I mumbled and noticed that he had a YouTube channel. He was sharing countless video clips on how he had built the winning speech, what it took to be a professional speaker.

Then, I found that he ran an online course, Stage Time University. Its faculty was composed of high-achievers: Mark Brown, Darren's speech coach, also a world champion of public speaking. Best-selling author and story consultant, Michael Hauge. World-class speech coaches, Michael Davis and Jennifer Leone. Kevin Burke and Stephanie Mchugh, both were sought after entertainers. It was clearly out of my league, but in a moment of absurdity, I clicked the join button.

I didn't know that it was one of the most critical moments of my life.

Stage Time University had an enormous collection of self-study materials. On top of them, there were interactive video coaching calls every Wednesday — an incredible chance to be coached by multiple, professional coaches. Excited, I jumped right in to find my message, something I could contribute to the world. Looking back, all of my stories were lacking in depth. Any of them could have been delivered by anyone else. All the coaches were trying to find the voice of me, encouraging me to go on. I purchased books they wrote, recommended, and studied them from cover to cover. My husband also gave me books about storytelling and writing guidebooks.

After a few coaching sessions, coach Jennifer Leone stopped me. She was connecting from her office in Australia, resting her chin on her hand, holding a pen. Her blonde hair touching her shoulders gently waved. She was wearing a white summer top while I bundled up in layers in the Pacific Northwest's chilly evening.

"Misako, I know you're always cheerful and enthusiastic, and you know we love you for that." She smiled. It warmed me in ways any jacket couldn't. We were over 7500 miles away, but she looked into my eyes as if she was sitting across a table. "I'm curious, though. Misako. Were you always cheerful like that?"

"Yes, I was, this is my —" A big lump clogged my throat. I choked and panicked. I'm a cheerful person, so people often asked me that very question. I had a go-to answer: "Yes, I was. This is my nature. As you can see, I'm such a goofball." I've said it countless times without thinking, but when she asked me the question while looking into my eyes, something happened in me. Nostalgia, fondness, and sadness — everything —

was bubbling up all over the place, with nowhere to go except out of my eyeballs. In front of the camera, with coaches and fellow students behind the screen, I wept. *What is going on with me?* I was surprised by my tears.

Another coach, Mark Brown, chimed in. "Would it be okay with you if we ask you more about your tears?" I nodded with a hiccup. "You might have an important story in there. The one you can speak from your heart. There's someone out there who needs to hear that story." He rubbed his shaved head and smiled. His smile was big, big enough to curl his nose and made me relaxed. I nodded and tried to say something, but all I could produce was a series of hiccups.

"All of you," Mark talked to the other attendees. "This is an important process to find your message, even though it's not comfortable."

I was thinking about Jennifer's question again. *Yes,* I thought. I was almost always cheerful because I chose to be. Sometimes it took effort, but I found that enthusiasm helped me to stay focused on the crucial matter. I liked to handle the challenges with a smile intact. I could have said that, but instead, I'd always described myself in a self-deprecating manner. In Japan, and wherever I lived, some people called me a "sweet summer child," one who's naïve and cannot understand how harsh life can be. I was okay with that because it represented my guard. I'd rather be misunderstood than expressing how I developed the skills. It would require sharing some of my painful pasts, and I was terrified by the idea. It was the first time that the tone of Jennifer's voice penetrated deeper than my guard; I found my wound, still raw.

Coach Michael Davis stepped in. "This is a safe place, Misako, but it's totally up to you. We all support you." His genuine smile reminded me of the reason I joined the coaching call, finding my message that can help others. I pushed myself to proceed.

My stomach churned as a childhood memory surfaced. I was a seventh-grader, and there was a speech contest. The teacher paired each boy with a girl to work in partnership. Girls were told to write a speech for their partner to deliver. That reflected the role of gender in society — women in the background being quietly supportive of men. I was paired with Akira, a shy straight-A student. We worked together, but just before the contest began, Akira ran to me, panting, "I —, I can't do this. You, you do this. You can do it, right? Right?" Akira was pale and fidgeting.

"Of course!" I said, and we ran to our teacher, Ms. Kakinuma, only to find this was a big mistake. Ms. Kakinuma erupted, Akira was forced to take the stage, and I was thrown out from the auditorium until all the speeches had been delivered.

With hiccuping and blowing my nose, I managed to squeeze out this portion of my story in the coaching call, used up all the hour.

After the session ended, I was staring at my monitor and thinking about the story. *There was more.* I was sure of it, but there was a dense fog blocking my memories. The mist swirled toward me, wraithlike, pulling me into itself. I shivered. *I don't want to do this. No, I don't want to go in there!* I stood up, walked away from my PC.

The more I thought about the memory, the more I was scared. Then, I started worrying if I was wasting the coaches' and attendees' time. What if I couldn't find my message? Worse, what if my message was useless? I wondered if I should cancel my membership so I could put the lid on the memories and be content with the way I was. *It might have been presumptuous of me to speak in public, anyway,* I thought. My mind was still meandering, and I was mindlessly roaming on Social media platforms.

"See you on the coaching call, Misako. You're getting there. Don't forget the Kleenex," Coach Michael replied to my thank you comment on his Facebook post. Then I realized that I didn't want to run away from my volatile emotions. I was reminded to align my heart and my action. I might cry, struggle, but I wanted to keep going until I did everything I could.

I decided to dig more into my childhood story. I proceeded through a speech delivery exercise, coached by Darren LaCroix and Kevin Burke. I was practicing the scene where Akira and I asked the teacher if we could switch roles. I started where Akira asked me to take the stage, and I accepted. Darren stopped me.

"Wait. I think you're rushing it through something important there." He stroked his chin, looked at me. "You wanted to take the stage, right? You wrote the speech, so you wanted to deliver it, correct?" Darren untangled my mess, pointed out my genuine desire. I nodded, realizing that I'd wanted to tell my story myself. With my voice. My gestures. I hated that I was stopped because of my gender.

"All right. Can you describe to me what Akira — Akira, right? Am I pronouncing it okay? Good. What did he look like?" Darren was listening to my description of Akira, leaning towards the camera. Then he rubbed the back of his neck and stood up. Just like that, an established, unmistakable charismatic man with blue eyes became a pencil-thin, fidgeting Asian boy with thick eyeglasses — Akira. I was brought to the corner of my school's auditorium. The musty odor, the draft, and the dusty sunbeams came into focus. Our teacher, Ms. Kakinuma, was facing the wall. Akira and I were looking up, talking to the back of her head and hoping she would turn around and approve our plans.

Then Kevin displayed Ms. Kakinuma for me. He started by showing his back and then sluggishly turned around. With one eyebrow raising higher than another, narrowed eyes, it wasn't Kevin anymore. All I saw was a middle-aged Asian woman in a beige cardigan with her hair tightly pulled back into a bun.

Ms. Kakinuma, who believed in teaching by fear and intimidation, was there. She approached me, and her face broke into red blotches as she took me by my arms and swung me up against the wall. An icy sensation ran through my spine. She lifted me, so her red eyes were in front of mine, too close. I was disoriented. She yelled, "You are a girl. Girls write. Boys take the stage. That's the rule!" I should have nodded, but I hurried to ask one question that I needed an answer.

"But, but, um, Akira doesn't want it, and I want it, so can we just — "

"ENOUGH!" She screamed, throwing me out of the auditorium. As I lost my balance and fell on my face, the door closed with a slam. The linoleum floor was cold and dusty on my left cheek. I sat up, wiped my face with my sleeve, shook my head. When I finally got up, I saw my long skinny shadow in front of me. The autumn sunlight poured in through the narrow windows.

"Are you okay?" Kevin asked me, and I came back to reality. I was shaking in front of my camera.

"Yes, um, yes, I'm fine, thank you," I said, and it was the end of the coaching call for the day.

After the call, my mind was back in the hall. Thirteen-year-old me was listening to the speeches through the gaps between the door and the wall. Akira was the last speaker. He sounded confident, and when it was over, he received huge applause. Ms. Kakinuma invited me back into the auditorium to watch the award ceremony. Akira was called to the podium and received the plastic trophy — we won first place. And then Akira called me from the stage. I jumped off the chair to join him but was yanked back by Ms. Kakinuma, who was holding my ponytail. The chair screeched as I was pulled back down, and everyone looked at us. Ms. Kakinuma stood up and pointed her finger at me, screaming: "Can you believe it? This girl wanted to go on the stage!"

Thunderous mocking laughter followed. I bit my lip, clenched my skirt, and tried to hold my anger.

After the contest adjourned, Ms. Kakinuma told me to stay. When most of the kids had left, she came closer to me.

"I'm going to teach you a lesson, so listen carefully. Do only what you are told to do, and you will be fine. For girls, the rules are different from boys. Get used to it," she pushed my forehead with her index finger and said, "Got it? No more stupid questions."

I stared at her, thinking, *aren't you supposed to make better rules for girls, as an adult woman?*

"I SAID, GOT IT?" Her voice and a slap came at the same time. I thought my eye had exploded. Then I saw stars. The slap was called *binta*, and it was commonly used as a punishment. I was supposed to apologize for making my teacher angry, but I didn't want to. I regained my balance, planted my feet wide apart, and glared at her. My fingernails were biting into my palms. She let out a big sigh, flapping the hand that had just hit me. "You are such a typical Fire-Horse, a piece of bad luck. You and your family will suffer!" she said, shooing me away.

I walked out of the auditorium, alone, and went straight to the woods I'd always cherished. I sat under my favorite oak tree on the fallen golden leaves. The first *kogarashi*, a cold wind, known as a harbinger of winter, blew the last leaves off the trees. At the time, Dad's business was also falling. It was the beginning of a series of family tragedies as if we were thrown into a raging river. Mom couldn't make it to the other side of the shore. I somehow believed Ms. Kakinuma, everything bad happened because of me. I was a piece of bad luck who would make everyone miserable. Her voice, the violent discipline she unleashed on me grabbed me tight. I started sobbing.

A couple of days later, I got a Facebook message from Kevin asking me to call him. Kevin was playing a live show every day, so I thought it could be some sort of mistake. I dialed the number given, anyway.

"Hey, Misako, oh, good!" Kevin answered, sounding relieved. It puzzled me.

"You know, we didn't have time to give you a technique to neutralize the scary memory. I left you with open wounds, and I felt bad."

"Oh goodness, you called me for that? How kind of you, thank you. Wow. ...Really?"

"Of course." Kevin chuckled.

"Here is what you can do," he said and started explaining one of the techniques.

"Think of something scary but laughable, something like— ah. Have you watched *Ghostbusters*?"

"Yes."

"Then you remember the Marshmallow Man, right?"

"Yes, that puffy one."

"That's right, the puffy one! That's the image you can hold on to. Make the teacher Marshmallow Man. Now try it. You won't be drawn into fear." He waited for me to create the images. The tightness came back in my stomach as I remembered her angry face, but it was loosening. Then, Ms. Kakinuma was plastered on the screen, no longer in my face.

"Did you get the image?"

"Yes, yes, I did," I said.

"Good. You've survived the experience, so it's your story to share. Whatever threatens you, you can always use this technique. All right?"

"Thank you, goodness, thank you," I couldn't help but repeat.

"See you at the coaching call," Kevin said and hung up the phone.

I let out a sigh and continued to think about Stage Time University. It wasn't "another online course;" it provided me with a sense of belongingness I was craving for.

All the warm words, support, and caring helped me gather enough strength to break the memory's cold grip. As the ice slipped away, I cried. The tears were like meltwater surging through a valley. It was a *good* cry. After the fear had dissolved, I was able to see the truth through a fresh pair of eyes. I'd wished to be true to myself — to break free of the expectations that society placed on me as a girl. I was too young, the culture was still too rigid, and my first attempt failed. As a thirteen-year-old girl, I concluded that I should adhere to everyone's expectations. It was the start of my struggles. Through marriage and career life, I was torn between selfhood and playing an expected role. I misunderstood, was convinced that being me was a selfish act.

My parents raised me to act outside of gender roles, even though Japanese society was strict about it. For instance, in any public grade school in those days, girls had to carry a red leather backpack. For boys, it was black. My parents gave me a custom-made backpack in my favorite color, blue. Blue was widely considered to be a boy color, but I didn't know that, and my parents didn't care. It became a big issue in the Parents Teacher Association, and my parents shook the meetings by demanding to know the reasons why my blue backpack was an issue. Following rules without questioning them was an important attitude in those days. Still, my parents were full of questions, and so was I. I could picture Ms. Kakinuma standing at a teacher's meeting, receiving criticisms because of a stubborn girl who never stopped questioning about rules. Such was the world we lived in. She'd probably been trying to prepare me, however misguidedly.

I must admit that I carried that fear and wrong beliefs into my adulthood. Furthermore, I long conflated "selfishness" with "being myself."

Being selfish is a state. It happens when we somehow believe the world *should* revolve around us. It stunts our growth. Being oneself is a process — it leads us to grow into our potential so that we can contribute our unique gift to the world. I let my confusion get the best of me for too long. Frustrated, I meandered and ended up hurting myself and the people I cared for. Sometimes, I must be vigilant of my preconceived biases and notions.

I still hate what Ms. Kakinuma did to me, and I probably always will, but I wouldn't say I hate her.

Spring Breeze

When I began to break free of the ice-cold grip, songbirds started serenading outside. In that spring, the owner sold the cabin we were renting. The landlord expected us to vacate the cabin in eighteen days from the date I received the letter. I had only two weekends to find a new place, pack up, and leave.

It was clear there was a misunderstanding of the tenant law on their side. I should have straightened it out calmly, but the idea of losing my place abruptly pushed me over the edge. The landlord quickly realized her mistake, apologized, and offered me to stay as long as I needed, but I didn't accept it. Everything felt like an old wet bandage; I wanted to rip it off with one yank and forget about it.

The cabin was furnished, so we didn't have many things, but again, my husband was out at sea, and it wasn't an easy task alone. Not only did I have to deal with frustration and fatigue, but an intense fear that kept bubbling up. I didn't know what I was afraid of exactly, but my head spun, my heart raced, and a cold sweat broke out. The fear was real: it was a panic attack.

I didn't sleep much, and I spent all night cleaning and packing before the eviction date. Everything was done when the sky started adding warmer shades — the morning was near. In my haze of exhaustion, I tripped over my own feet and fell on my purse. A tangerine was in there, and squishing under my palm, the fragrant citrus mist sprayed out.

I gasped. The scent revealed a long-cloaked memory, and I

became a teenager again.

I was in the car with my family. It was shortly after we'd given up Mom's dream home. We loaded Dad's car with our belongings—as much as we could squeeze in—and visited our relatives one by one. None of them took us in. We were roaming around from one place to another, staying in the car. *When was it?*—it was a wet and windy day in November. Dad was driving, Mom was next to him, and Takuya sat beside me in the back. I was in my school uniform, pressing my cheek to the window. A lighthouse under the gray sky came into view. It was Inubo Lighthouse, where I'd been born. The winds were howling, and I could hear the waves pounding the cliff. Dad drove into the parking lot. He parked in front of the warning signs.

DO NOT ENTER.

STOP.

NO U-TURN BEYOND THIS POINT.

Beyond the sign, there was no land.

"Well." Dad parked the car and turned off the engine. The wind died down, and fog crept up from the cliff. Takuya and I looked at each other, wondering if we were to get out.

"Oh, we still have these." Mom dug into her tote bag and brought up a plastic bag, two tangerines in it. Takuya received the bag and asked me, "Which one do you want?"

"That one," I pointed at a smaller one.

"Oki-Doki. Hey, do you want me to peel it for you?" Takuya

said as he handed one.

"I can peel it myself now. Watch," I said, and put my thumb on the waxy orange skin. When I decided where to dig, Dad said, "After eating, we're going to drive into the ocean. We'll all do it together." I rested my thumb on the fruit. There was something different in Dad's voice. It was lower, monotone, and tremulous. He always spoke with confidence, and now he sounded like a stranger. The voice sent a chill down my spine.

Dad added that he could drive over the fence if we were brave enough. He was suggesting *muri-shinju*, parent-child suicide — common enough to have a formal name. In the Japanese press, reports of *muri-shinju* could be found at least once or twice per month. Japanese society wasn't forgiving when one failed to live up to one's obligations, especially in bringing disgrace to their family name. Despite encompassing murder, the crime was often reported sympathetically.

Dad was raised, almost brainwashed, to believe that preserving family honor was the highest priority, even if it meant sacrificing his own life — and ours. In his mind, his wife and children were extensions of himself. It was a die-hard tradition belonging to a man who'd descended from a samurai family.

"Don't worry. It will be quick. I promise. We'll all be free from the shame." Dad let it out in one breath. Then he turned to Mom and said, "We have no choice."

I was sure Dad had no doubt that Mom would nod with her calm smile, as she always did.

"No!" She screamed instead and gave me a jump. Mom had never raised her voice to anyone, and it was the only time she did so in front of us.

"Are you telling us that you've given up? Uh-uh, no. NO! I don't believe you!" Dad widened his eyes, with his mouth semi-opened. He took a moment before continuing.

"Listen, honey. I've dishonored my family. You saw their faces, right? I can't let us live a life of shame. I want to leave with at least a shred of dignity. This is the only way out." Dad leaned toward her and put his hand on her lap.

"That," Mom stammered and shook her head. She took a deep breath and restarted. "That doesn't sound like my husband." Her voice was calm again.

"My husband always found a workaround. You always have. That's who you are. The never give up guy, right? No one can take the man from you." She placed her hand on Dad's. Dad looked at her and closed his mouth.

"You are not done yet. We are not." Her eyes held strength.

"You don't understand." Dad pulled his hand away from her and turned his face to the sea of gray. He gripped the steering wheel with both hands, and the leather steering cover squeaked. Mom was staring at him. Her lips zipped, and her fingers laced in prayer on her lap.

Dad shook his head, started the engine, and Takuya crushed the tangerine in his hands. The citrus scent filled the car. Not a word from anyone. No one moved. I stared at the juice oozing out between Takuya's fingers and dripping down from his fists. My heart was drumming, making my entire body vibrate with a throbbing headache. Everything became blurry.

"Yeah, okay." Dad let out a big sigh and turned his face to Mom. He took another deep breath.

"You're right. I'm not done yet. I'm still your never-give-up-guy," he said. Mom nodded, letting out a small sigh and sank into the seat. Dad looked at us through the rearview mirror. "You two knew it was a joke, right?" Takuya nodded and tossed the crushed fruit into the plastic bag. He then pulled a handkerchief from his back pocket. I was staring at Takuya's shaking hands, trying to unfold his wrinkled, blue-gray handkerchief. We left the lighthouse, drove down to the city.

A chorus of songbirds returned to my ears. Wrens were singing their hearts out, and soon they were joined by song sparrows. The morning glow had lifted the darkness. Gentle light leaped through the window.

I noticed the lilac trees were blooming. Mom cherished the lilac tree we had in front of our house, and then it hit me—I'd become older than she ever was. It had been decades since she left. I'd spent more of my life without her than with her. I dropped my head between my knees.

"Mom," I said and shut my eyes, squeezing tightly to hold back the tears.

I felt the gentle touch on my back—Mom's soft palm. I could picture her delicate fingers with their almond-shaped nails, always neatly trimmed.

"I'm exhausted. I can't get up." Tears rolled down my cheeks.

I heard Mom's voice. "Of course you can."

"I need you, Mom."

"Oh, shush," she chuckled. "You haven't needed me for a long time now." Her voice was as calm and warm as I remembered.

"It wasn't easy, Mom. I didn't want pity or sympathy, so I tried really hard to stay ahead, and, and—." I felt her hugging me.

"You've found the strength," she said.

"I'm not sure about that now. I still crumble like this."

"True strength doesn't mean you never break down. It means getting back up when you do. *Nanakorobi Yaoki*, remember?"

Nanakorobi Yaoki means to fall seven times and rise eight. No matter how many times you get knocked down, you get up again—it's a Japanese concept of resilience.

"Yes, I do, and that's why I didn't give up on myself. I wanted to make you proud, even after you left. I still do, Mom."

"I know, sweetie. I know," she said. My sobbing slowly subsided.

In some corner of my brain, I was aware this was all a dream. I would wake up soon, alone. So I squeezed my eyes even tighter.

"What's on your mind, Misako?"

"I was wondering if you were... happy."

"Oh, my little sweetie pie. I think you know the answer."

"But, Mom, what if we were..."

"Stop right there." Her voice was gentle, yet firm. "Don't get caught up in wishing for a better past. Focus on the things you can do something about, sweetie. You don't know how many tomorrows you will get."

I took a deep breath against the pain — thinking about her last few months of life in poverty pierced my heart.

"All right, sweetie," she said. "If you need to hear it from me, yes, I was the happiest person in the world."

"Even with all the hard things we've been through?"

"Especially for those," she said. "I'm proud of how I handled them. I did pretty well when I convinced your dad not to end our lives, didn't I? I should get an award." Her voice contained her smile.

If it wasn't for her, I could have been mentioned in a small-town newspaper article as a victim of a family suicide.

"You gave me a second chance."

"You deserved it. We all did," she said.

"Go all out, Misako. You're tougher than you think. You can handle so much more than others tell you. Be *genki*, spread your enthusiasm. If they can't appreciate who you are, they don't deserve to have you," she said.

I nodded.

"That's my girl." Mom's voice was fading. I lifted my head to see her smile one more time, but there was only the sunlit window in front of me. The native Pacific Rhododendron flowers were poking through the bushes behind the lilac trees.

It was hard to believe that snow and ice had covered the ground just a few months ago. The seasons change without fail. Life, too, has its seasons — things change. Not all changes are ones we choose, but we can grow with challenges and nurture our new growth. No matter what happens, life is beautiful — and short.

I got up, remembering how Mom had helped me stand straight and tall when the weight of the world tried to press me down. I walked out of the cabin. As I closed the door one last time, a bumblebee flew by with a heavy buzz, headed to the lilac tree. The spring breeze followed, carrying giggling sounds from the swallows. I smiled at the sky.

Epilogue

My father owned a Japanese sword, a *katana*, that had been passed down to him through generations. It was displayed in the *tokonoma*, a recessed space in our Japanese-style reception room. No one else was allowed to touch it.

I still remember the *katana*. Even though I was very young, I could sense there was something special about it. It's been said that a samurai's sword is his soul.

Katana making is an intricate process. A chunk of steel is burned in high heat by the master swordsmiths, pulled out to be hammered, quenched in cold water, and put back into the flame. These steps remove impurities from the metal and strengthen the build. Many such cycles later, the forged blade reveals its strength and beauty, becomes one of a kind — *katana*. This process of transforming was often used as a metaphor for personal development in my family. Just like the *katana*, we, too, awaken the real strength within us through adversity, we were told.

My father's *katana* had a couple of battle scars.

"These are honorable scars. They show it's fought and survived," he said.

Every scar you have is a reminder that you've survived the pain and the suffering. You've endured. You've made it through. You now have a deeper understanding and greater compassion toward others' struggles.

You and I both know that a pain-free life doesn't exist, but we can always choose the right pain — the pain that helps us grow. The kind that leaves a scar that we can be proud of.

Take heart, my friend! You are stronger than you think.

The 5-Step GENKI Method

The 5-Step GENKI Method

This five-step plan is designed to keep adversity in perspective. Each step is a reminder that while we can't control everything in our lives, we can decide how we respond. And the choices we make will determine the kind of person we grow into.

G: Get Some Breathing Room (When Life Ambushes You)

A focused mind brings out the best in you. A scattered brain can generate out-of-the-box creative ideas. A panicky state, however, isn't your friend as you and I both know. When the mind is spinning, "thinking" doesn't function as well as it should, so pay attention to your body. Most likely, your breathing is shallow and fast. If you're like me, when your breathing is shallow, your thoughts stay shallow. So try to breathe deeply and slowly. Once you get the lovely deep breaths, it gets easier to give your mind a direction: find your strength to get back to yourself, your calmer state. Yes, it's hard to remember what to do when life ambushes you. You'll need to come up with a short phrase to take a moment for yourself. You're more than welcome to use my mantra to find your strength: Stop. Breathe. Channel your inner samurai (or your hero).

E: Embrace Who You Are Becoming (When You Wonder, "Now What?")

You've been taught to follow the rules and color inside the lines. You might have been conditioned to think in certain ways—and you think that's who you "should" be. If you genuinely believe that's who you are, great! If not, it's time to question everything you've been told. You're NOT here to fulfill someone else's expectation. Be curious about your life: spend some time to find out who you are. Better yet, *decide* who you want to become. Find your purpose, find your "why"—all helpful, but in the end, your decision is the one that makes a difference in your life. If you feel lost or not sure where to start, I recommend taking some well-known and trusted personality tests for a start (don't stop there, though). We are too close to ourselves, sometimes those tests help you see your strength and weakness. Below are a few examples:

Myers Briggs Personality Type Indicator by the Myers & Briggs Foundation (https://www.myersbriggs.org/my-mbti-personality-type/mbti-basics/)

16Personalities.com by NERIS Analytics (free version available)

CliftonStrengths by Gallup (https://www.gallup.com/clifton-strengths/en/home.aspx).

Those personality tests are indicators; they don't define you unless you let them. So, whatever the results are, pick what you can take pride in. It's your life, it's your decision. What others think of you is none of *your* business. Focusing on your choices, how you see yourself.

N: Navigate through Changes (When You Start Something New and Confusing)

Change always brings challenges. Everything is weird until you get used to it; it's only natural to feel anxious. You should be proud of yourself, putting yourself out of your comfort zone! You just need to take charge of your mind. Facing a challenge is much easier than being chased by it. So, try saying this to yourself: "Bring it on!" It gives your mind the right direction. Accept reality as is instead of wishing for a different situation. Important to remember: accepting a situation doesn't equate to giving up; you're acknowledging the facts. It helps you to plan/prepare for the next move. Be creative whenever possible, and adjust as needed. The truth is often somewhere in the discovery process, and the rewards are boundless.

K: Be Kind to Yourself (When Your Inner Voice Attacks You)

Treat yourself as if you're your own good friend, especially when you're full of doubt. You and I both know that the blame game—including blaming yourself—never helps. Make an effort to catch yourself when your inner negativities get louder. Ask yourself: Is criticizing myself helping me now? Would I say this if I were talking to my good friend?

Imagine what you would say if your good friend were beating herself up about something. You would stop her adding extra pain, right? Good friends provide comfort and care, and they push each other to grow. We thrive when we are surrounded by supportive people. Be a good friend to yourself. You deserve it.

I: Integrate Who You Are with How You Live (This Is Your Life)

One of the biggest mistakes I made was being convinced that being myself was a selfish act. Oscar Wilde once said, "Selfishness is not living as one wishes to live. It is asking other people to live as one wishes to live." Being selfish stunts your growth. Being oneself lets you grow into our potential so that we can contribute our unique gift to the world. Align your heart and your actions, and celebrate uniqueness!

***

I can almost hear you saying, "This all sounds good, but aren't those steps all too simple? Everything is easier said than done!" Yes, you are right. Each step is simple, but let me remind you that simple doesn't always mean easy. Most of them need some work and take time, but I can promise you this—it's worth the effort. To practice, I made a bonus workbook for you.

Grab your bonus here: https://takeheart.misakoyoke.com/wp/take-heart-bonus/

Or scan the QR code below

Now, Your Turn

Storytelling is a powerful tool that connects us on a deeper level. It does take some strength to be open about ourselves and our struggles, but it's worth the effort. Our life stories can provide comfort to others facing similar challenges by reducing their sense of isolation.

Now it's your turn to share your experiences and pass on your wisdom. Start gathering your memories, good or bad, type them up to develop your story. Each of us is a work in progress—sharing our stories will help each other. Your story can inspire and encourage others. In return, you can be inspired and encouraged.

Please share, whenever, wherever it's appropriate. If you'd like to know how to turn your memories into a story, it'll be my pleasure to work with you. Please visit my website: misakoyoke.com for more information.

P.S.

Thank you for investing your time with this book. It means SO much to me if you could take a quick few minutes to review this book online, wherever you feel comfortable.

Of course, I'd be happy to hear from you via email. It's totally up to you. Tell me more: misakoyoke.com/take-heart-your-voice

Or scan the QR code below

Acknowledgment

I'd like to start by thanking my husband, Jonathan. I know compliments make you cringe, so I keep it short: I'm glad you're not the superstitious type.

To all my friends from all over the world, you've heard me say, "I love you," many times. I hope you know I always mean it I also want to thank everyone, whoever supported me *or* helped me grow.

I want to shout, "Arigato!" to my best friends Satoka, Chizuko, and Akiko. I will probably cry when we get together again.

To Lia, Ioasa, Lani, Ioasa Jr, and Miracle—my Samoan *aiga, fa'afetai lava* for everything.

To my mentors and coaches of public speaking: Veda Moline and Joe Miller, you gave me the start I needed. Thank you.

To Darren LaCroix, 2001 world champion of Public speech, and the founder of Stage Time University. It's beyond my words to express how grateful I am to you.

Stage time University's Coaches: Jennifer Leone, a world-class speech coach from Australia. Michael Davis, also a world-class speech coach. Mark Brown, 1995 world champion of public speaking, also Darren's speech coach. Michael Hauge, best-seller author and story consultant, thank you for guiding me to find my voice. Kevin Burk, and Stephanie Mchugh, both professional entertainers. Thank you all for spending your valuable time supporting me. Even thouhg you all trained me to speak up, and I've learned a lot, I still become speechless when I try to express my gratitude.

STU's *Write it Right Now* Instructors Maureen Zappala and Sheryl Green, you pushed my book writing project forward. Vickie Nickel, Regine MacDonald, and Patti Marler, extremely caring STU team. Fellow STU students and alumni. Thank you for being so patient with me!

To Maxwell Anderson, you're such a talented and driven editor. As cliché as it may sound, this book wouldn't exist without your help. Thank you.

I'd like to express my gratitude to all my book creation team at AAE, Thank you.

To Mom, Dad, and my big bro Takuya, his wife Akemi. All of you left the earth in a hurry. I know it's too late, but thank you. I love you. I'll live my life well, I promise.

Recommendation

Public Speaking and Business:

Stage Time University: https://stagetimeuniversity.com/

Books

Storytelling Made Easy by Michael Hauge

Writing Life Stories by Bill Roorbach

The Anatomy of Story by John Truby

The Book on Writing by Paula LaRocque

The Emotion Thesaurus: A Writer's Guide to Character Expression by Angela Ackerman and Becca Puglisi.

Speaking and Storytelling

TOMstorytellersLab.com

This is where you'll see me online often, working with business professionals, Tim Barnaby and Oscar Romero. We also offer coaching services, teaching storytelling techniques to help you share your personal story in an impactful way. Any questions are welcome: Ask@TOMstoryTellersLab.com

Looking forward to hearing your stories!

Endnotes

1   https://pubmed.ncbi.nlm.nih.gov/1052742/
2   https://www.nytimes.com/1987/01/15/world/japan-s-zo-diac-66-was-a-very-odd-year.html
3   Ode to the West Wind by Percy Bysshe Shelley
4   http://www.loyalbooks.com/book/Bushido-Soul-of-Japan

Use The Following Pages For Your Story

You have stories in you. Let your story unfold, and find your authentic self through your stories.

Please remember: When you're reday to share, I'm all ears.
I can be reached at: takeheart@misakoyoke.com

Made in the USA
Las Vegas, NV
17 September 2021